In the Best Interest of the
Child

Also by Stanton E. Samenow

Before It's Too Late

Inside the Criminal Mind

Straight Talk About Criminals

Coauthored with Samuel Yochelson

The Criminal Personality: A Profile for Change

The Criminal Personality: The Change Process

The Criminal Personality: The Drug User

In the Best Interest of the Child

How to Protect Your Child from the Pain of Your Divorce

Stanton E. Samenow, Ph.D.

 Crown Publishers / New York

Copyright © 2002 by Stanton E. Samenow, Ph.D.

Published by Crown Publishers, New York, New York.
Member of the Crown Publishing Group.

Random House, Inc. New York, Toronto, London, Sydney, Auckland
www.randomhouse.com

CROWN is a trademark and the Crown colophon is a registered trademark
of Random House, Inc.

Printed in the United States of America

DESIGN BY LENNY HENDERSON

Library of Congress Cataloging-in-Publication Data
Samenow, Stanton E., 1941–
In the best interest of the child : how to protect your child from the pain of
your divorce / Stanton E. Samenow. — 1st ed.
1. Children of divorced parents—United States—Psychology.   2. Divorced
parents—United States—Psychology.   3. Divorce—United States—
Psychological aspects.   4. Custody of children—United States.   I. Title.
HQ777.5 .S25   2002
306.89—dc21   2001042468

ISBN 0-8129-3189-0

10 9 8 7 6 5 4 3 2 1

First Edition

To the domestic relations attorneys with whom I have had the privilege to work in the Virginia jurisdictions of the City of Alexandria and the Counties of Arlington, Fairfax, Loudoun, and Prince William.

To the conscientious, devoted, and wise judges before whom I have had the honor of testifying in custody matters in the domestic relations and circuit courts in the Virginia jurisdictions of the City of Alexandria and the Counties of Arlington, Fairfax, Loudoun, and Prince William.

Acknowledgments

I WISH TO THANK Dr. David Cohen, Ed Schuman, and Richard and Sybille Stromberg for the excellent suggestions they offered after reading and rereading the manuscript. Thanks also to Betsy Ferry and Jeremy Herbst for their ideas and assistance. I appreciate the help of Martin A. Gannon, Attorney at Law, who reviewed some of the legal material and suggested additional resources. And, finally, thanks to David D. Masterman, Attorney at Law, for reviewing material pertaining to different types of custody arrangements.

Contents

Introduction

Do not despair as you read this book! A great deal of it will seem unbelievable, shocking, or depressing as I tell you what parents do to each other and their children as they pursue custody. Even loving, well-intentioned parents lose perspective in the emotional turbulence of divorce—and it's always the children who pay the highest price. But separation, divorce, and resolving child custody need not wreck everyone's lives. There are ways to minimize the grief, anxiety, frustration, anger, and dissipation of resources. If you know what to avoid and if you take the positive steps I recommend, you can spare your child and yourself an enormous amount of suffering. You can act in the best interest of your child.

I've been an independent custody evaluator for the last seventeen years. Courts or attorneys appoint me not to represent the divorcing mother or father but to act as a neutral, independent professional whose role is to recommend what's best for the child. I've interviewed children and their parents before, during, and after divorce proceedings. I've also spoken with grandparents, teachers, friends, therapists, and other concerned individuals. In short, I've seen your child's world from perspectives you've never seen. The things I've seen happen to kids are what compelled me to write this book.

I have witnessed the casualties as parents fight each other for custody of their children. Boys and girls are thrown into turmoil when their family life unravels. Caught in the cross fire, they are reluctant to take sides for fear of appearing disloyal to either parent.

I've seen parents stop at nothing in their attempts to defeat each other, including using their sons and daughters as pawns. I recall a mother and father referring to the transfer of their daughter from one house to the other as the hostage exchange. I know two other parents who decided one full year after their divorce that the only way to avoid open warfare was to meet in front of a police station to pick up or deliver their two-year-old! I've seen children cry because their birthday party was canceled when a parent planned a competing event and failed to notify the other parent. I've heard of boys and girls tearfully refusing to visit a parent, then being taken forcibly. I can't count the number of times I've heard about one parent berating the other in front of their child because the youngster was returned just a few minutes late.

When a judge or the attorneys for the parents ask me to participate in these civil cases, it's almost always because the proceedings have hit rock bottom. The litigants are being anything but civil to each other. Marriage counseling has failed, mediation has failed, and even litigation has so far not resolved what would be in the best interest of the child.

Let me tell you how, as a clinical psychologist, I became involved in the area of child custody and visitation, which has occupied me for nearly seventeen years. In 1978, I opened my practice of clinical psychology. Until then I was chief psychologist in the Program for the Investigation of Criminal Behavior at St. Elizabeths Hospital in Washington, D.C. My specialty was the evaluation and counseling of adult and juvenile offenders sent to me through the courts, referred by various agencies, or dragged to my office by distraught family members. I have written books about criminal thinking and behavior and have presented speeches and workshops for professionals throughout the United States and Canada. I've acted as an expert witness in courts regarding criminal sentencing.

In 1984, a judge asked me to take a case quite different from any I had handled before. It was a child custody dispute in which allegations, including those of sexual abuse, were flying. I was to conduct an evaluation and make recommendations to the court. To my surprise, I discovered that this case and many subsequent ones had much in common with my work with criminals. Regrettably, I've found the very thought processes and behavior characteristic of the criminal personality in many parents who single-mindedly pursue their objective to "win" custody at any cost and, in the process, hurt those they profess to love most—their own children.

In my writings on the criminal personality, I've described in detail the thinking and behavior patterns of individuals who pursue any means to an end. They rarely put themselves in the place of others, are untruthful and unrelenting in their efforts to control other people, harbor unrealistic expectations, and frequently fail to consider what will be beneficial or harmful to others. Ferreting out and preying upon vulnerability, they leave a trail of emotional, financial, and physical destruction. When held accountable, these victimizers claim that they are not at fault and blame others.

Of course, I am not suggesting that all parents who seek custody of their children think and behave like criminals, but usually the parents I encounter have ceased being reasonable and are engaged in protracted warfare with each other. Stating the best of intentions, these mothers and fathers have become so enmeshed in battle that they have lost sight of the needs of their children. They resort to subterfuge, engage in machinations to build themselves up at the expense of the other spouse, and demonstrate tunnel vision.

In all the situations I encounter, the marriage is over. The parents may still be living in the same house, or each may have his or her own residence. In the best of circumstances, both parents want to talk to me to work out a way both can be involved in their child's life. The mother and father want to avoid conflict, not create it. They don't question each other's fitness, devotion, or competence as a parent. But in most of my cases, unfortunately, the situation is far more contentious. One or both parents are referred by a domestic relations attorney and are gearing up to litigate. There may be no legal custody arrangement, or the court may have ordered a temporary arrangement (pendente lite, as it is called). The child is likely to be shuttling between Mom and Dad. The atmosphere is hostile.

Whether the parents come to me prepared to be reasonable or determined to eviscerate each other, they have one thing in common: *They always declare that they wish to spare their child turmoil and trauma.* Initially, most are sincere about protecting their child, but their sensitivity diminishes if there is a custody war. Even when their parents' separation and divorce are relatively amicable, children suffer as family life changes forever and they are forced to adapt to a situation not of their own making. They fare much worse if their parents' divorce is contentious.

You are doubtless reading this book in crisis. You, too, declare that you want to spare your child turmoil and trauma. You'll mean it when you say it, but I promise you that divorce proceedings can and will test your resolve. I've written this book to help you keep your promise to yourself and to your child. I'll discuss the difficulties that parents and children encounter as the family breaks up. By describing numerous pitfalls and how to avoid them, I will help you protect your child during a traumatic time.

I

The Demise of Family Life

DURING WARFARE OVER child custody, were you to ask the parents about their motives, each would contend that he or she is acting in their child's best interest. This assertion likely would be followed by withering criticism of the other parent. Two human beings who vowed to spend their lives together have become the bitterest of enemies. By the time these parents are litigants in a custody battle, they can hardly recall what qualities attracted them to each other. In fact, even when pressed neither may be able to come up with any positive statement about his or her spouse.

The threat by one parent to destroy the other in some fashion is not necessarily empty. I have seen it happen, psychologically and financially. During protracted warfare parents imperil their health, their jobs, their relationships, and, of course, their children's sense of security and well-being. To finance custody battles, parents have depleted their savings, dipped into retirement funds, invaded their children's college accounts, secured second mortgages, and borrowed from their own families.

How much of an impact does your divorce have on your kids?

On the one hand, some experts claim that living through a family breakup invariably results in permanent psychological scars. The opposite camp of experts believe that little lasting damage is done because children are amazingly resilient. Realistically, the impact depends on the dynamics of your family and the psychological makeup of your child.

I have found that, no matter what the situation, children are hurt when the two human beings upon whom they depend most part company. I have yet to encounter a case of divorce in which the offspring do not experience intense sadness, considerable anxiety, and confusion. No matter how resilient he may appear, no child is immune to suffering during a family breakup, even if he remains materially comfortable, continues to perform well in school, and spends time with each of two devoted parents.

An intelligent, poised, and unusually mature thirteen-year-old girl whose parents had separated seemed to be handling her situation with little difficulty. She remained an honor roll student, had lots of friends, and was able to continue living in the family home with her mother and sister while spending regular periods of time with her father. The school counselor told me that, other than what he learned from the parents, he never would have suspected anything was awry at home. This child was adept at hiding her misery. Near tears, she told me that more than anything else she wanted to spend equal time with her mom and dad. The issue wasn't so much the division of time but missing the life she had known for most of her thirteen years. She was very aware of her parents' conflicts, but these meant little to her. As she pointed out, these were *their* differences with each other, and she was not part of that. She lived with and loved both and, as children do, took for granted that every day she would live in one home with her mother and her father. She resented having to divide her time between two homes and grieved losing the family that she regarded as the bedrock of her existence.

Was this young adolescent traumatized for life by her parents' divorce? I doubt it. She still had strong relationships with both parents, who were psychologically sensitive and did their best to help and support her. She was able to remain in the same neighborhood and attend the same school, and she was afforded the opportunity to discuss her problems with a skilled therapist. Despite these favorable circumstances, unanswered questions remain: What loyalty issues did she inwardly contend with? To what extent was her trust in her parents and other adults shaken? If the two adults who were her anchor had let her down, could she feel confident that any relationship could survive conflict? How did her parents' divorce affect her hope of one day finding a mate and having a family?

Of course, children of divorced parents do develop enduring relationships, marry, and raise families. Unarguably, the emotional toll is likely to be highest when parents continually involve their youngsters in adult conflicts. The losses are more bearable and the damage less when parents set aside their personal vendettas and cooperate in making decisions that affect their children. The focus of this book is how, during separation and divorce, you can reduce stress, minimize suffering, and behave in a manner that truly is in the best interest of your child. You may flinch at the horror stories you're about to read, but I've included them to sensitize you so that you can avoid denial and sidestep hurtful mistakes. Later in the book I will discuss the much preferred alternatives.

Chapter 1

Divorce and Separation: Toxic Patterns

In case after case of divorce I've seen, differences over money, in-laws, sex, child rearing, religion, and other matters took their toll. The critical issue wasn't that such differences existed. Rather the personalities of the spouses determined whether conflicts would get resolved.

A discussion of the many reasons for divorce would require an entire book. My intent here is to identify the most common themes and patterns I've encountered during my years of conducting custody evaluations. Understanding the themes of your own marriage and dissolution can give you insights into the expectations you brought into the relationship and what you think should happen now that the marriage is over.

Most of the men and women I've interviewed didn't rush into marriage. Because they had known their partners for years, they were pretty confident about their decision to marry. One of the nastiest divorces I encountered involved two people who knew each other nearly a decade before they married. In many instances these adults were in love with the idea of being married more than they were with each other. The mere state of being married fulfilled im-

4

portant psychological needs. It enhanced their self-image because someone had found them attractive. Marriage alleviated their loneliness. For men and women still emotionally or financially tied to their parents, it provided liberation. By getting married some could delay grappling with decisions about education and career.

Some seemed drawn by a particular characteristic of a partner that so dominated their perception of the person that they overlooked a lot of qualities that later took their toll on the marriage. When sex became the early focus of the relationship, some couples mistook physical compatibility for overall compatibility. Some regarded marriage as a stepping-stone to higher social and economic status. They married to move up the rungs of the ladder, not to find a soul mate.

Some confused shared goals with shared values. They could agree that they both wanted to have children, live in a comfortable home, and share an active social life. Not until they actually had a young child and were coping with the demands of a job and tending to routine chores did they make dismaying discoveries. Agreeing to have a child was easy, but agreeing on how to raise that child was impossible. In some cases by the time a parent discovered the demands of bringing up children, he already had become so immersed in ego-gratifying activities outside the home that he was reluctant to give them up. His spouse resented being saddled with the drudgery at home as a virtual single parent.

The typical divorce story is that two people who thought they had everything in common eventually discover they share very little. Having gradually established separate lives with their own activities and friends, they become resentful of each other. Asked how this came to be, these men and women often tell me that their partner turned out to be very different from the person they originally married; they were baffled and distressed by the change. However, the idea that somehow their partner had changed so much was largely an illusion allowing them to shift the focus to their spouse rather than consider that they had erred in their perceptions or had had unrealistic expectations.

In many instances unrealistic expectations had doomed the relationship from the beginning. For example, adults who enter marriage with strong unresolved dependency needs may drive a partner away. This occurs when a very dependent person constantly looks to another to gain self-confidence. In the early stages of the relationship, the fit between the two seems ideal. The more independent, confident partner feels needed and valued. And the dependent partner has found a tower of strength who will help him or her feel more secure and worthwhile. But a neurotic cycle ensues in which the dependent spouse makes incessant demands and doesn't feel complete unless validated by the other. The spouse on the receiving end feels more and more at a loss; sensing that he or she can never fulfill the needs of the spouse, the more independent partner becomes frustrated, depressed, or angry and may back away. Feeling abandoned and resentful, the dependent partner becomes even more demanding. Many years may pass before one or both realize that the marriage is unworkable. The couple may never really understand why things haven't worked out, and the marriage ends in bitterness.

Characteristics of their partner that originally appealed to these men and women sometimes turned out to be liabilities. A number of women had been attracted by men who seemed decisive, ambitious, and ready to take charge of any situation. Later, they realized that the strength they admired was an attempt to control them.

Anne had envisioned a traditional marriage in which her husband would be the breadwinner and she would stay home and raise their children. Attracted initially by Roy's charismatic personality, she began to feel trapped because Roy seemed to have turned into a dictator. In fact, he had always been a controller; it just took a few years for Anne to see him this way. On most matters she acquiesced in what he wanted because she didn't like confrontations. But when we met, Anne told me she couldn't bear living with him any longer. "He has an ugly personality. I was to take on all the traditional roles. My friends weren't good enough. I couldn't see this one or that one. My sister invited me out for my birthday. He said, 'How many other whores are going?' "

Although she was Methodist, Anne had agreed to raise their four children Roman Catholic, since that was Roy's faith. This concession meant little to him, for he would have no part in their parochial school education. While Roy slept each morning, Anne drove the car pool and attended school-related activities without him. She noted, "Not until I nagged and whined and bitched did he get up earlier so he could pour cereal into a bowl." To show her children the church she grew up in, Anne took them to one Methodist service, making Roy furious.

Attempting to regulate nearly every aspect of Anne's existence, Roy was scathingly critical of her dependency. She recalled, "I was told all I wanted was a free ride." Desiring to do something worthwhile on her own and contribute to the family's finances, Anne started a tutoring business. With pride she said, "I made more money per hour than I ever made." But Roy told her she was wasting her time and neglecting chores at home.

Some divorcing husbands and wives failed to realize that a successful marriage requires effort. When marital differences emerged they yelled at each other but didn't work to resolve the differences. Resentment festered, and the relationship suffered. Since they'd never developed a successful way to address conflict, they simply stopped communicating. Some made a perfunctory try at marriage counseling but quickly concluded there was no hope. Others thought they could maintain the marriage as long as they had a relationship on the side that provided some compensation.

One father told me that he had had "a great marriage" for years. He said that he could find no flaw in his wife, who had been faithful and seemed satisfied with their relationship. When I asked him why, if the marriage was so good, he embarked upon an affair, he replied, "It wasn't enough. Something was missing. I tried to put my finger on it. I don't know. I don't know if it was the excitement of having an affair. It was exciting to have someone want you." It turned out that this man's disaffection had very little to do with his spouse. He was an excitement junkie, perpetually dissatisfied with whatever he had. Instead of working to resolve difficulties or improve a situation, he sought illicit excitement to juice up his life. His wife and children were the victims.

For some divorcing couples, having children crystallized their differences. Roger reported that Judi was thrilled at becoming pregnant. But not long after she gave birth the marital relationship changed drastically. Judi said that Roger seemed more married to his own parents than to her; he frequently called them, relied on their opinions about the baby's care, and ignored what she thought. "His family is the main priority," she told me. "It didn't seem that way when we were dating. He now goes to his parents about everything."

When a physician recommended that their child have surgery, Roger ran to his parents for advice even though his father-in-law was a pediatrician. As the couple nitpicked at each other and quarreled over their child, they concluded that they had been dead wrong in believing that they shared similar values. They couldn't even agree on where to live, each insisting upon purchasing a home near his or her parents. Neither of these adults had moved beyond strong emotional dependence on his or her parents. Having a child made no difference. Neither Judi nor Roger was prepared to establish a life without the shelter of parents nearby.

Some divorcing parents contended that their marriage disintegrated because one spouse was happy to be the child's playmate but shirked the more tedious aspects of child rearing. Many mothers complained they had to do it all, even if they worked outside the home. They acknowledged that their spouse entertained their child very well but rarely changed a diaper, fed or bathed the baby, or got up with the youngster at night. As soon as a child fussed, the father handed him back. Although it is not unusual for mothers to be more involved with infants, for these couples, infancy marked the beginning of a pattern of noninvolvement that became entrenched as the youngster got older. Feeling taken for granted and used, the mothers resented their husbands' refusal to be partners in child rearing.

It's important to recognize how your misperceptions and frustrated expectations have contributed to the end of your marriage, because I've found that these same patterns perpetuate themselves through divorce proceedings and their aftermath.

Separation: A New Set of Problems

When you decided to separate, you traded one set of difficulties for another. Even though you're no longer living under the same roof, you still must contend with each other. You're forever linked through your children, and you'll always need to make certain decisions jointly. Your personalities are unlikely to change, but problems and decisions will. Some divorcing couples will establish a cooperative, civil relationship. Others will remain at war for years.

Your initial marital separation probably didn't require a custody order. However, during the months before a court hearing, the wrangling may be endless. A routine matter can become surprisingly complicated. When you were together, you could somehow juggle your child's school, Scouts, religious activities, sports, and whatever else he or she was involved in. Living apart, you guard your time with the child and don't want all the car pooling and after-school activities to usurp it.

One father was irate that most of his Wednesday time was consumed by soccer practice, leaving him only an hour and a half before he had to drive his son back to the boy's mother's home. He snapped, "My wife just signs him up for whatever, and I have to follow along." His wife thought her husband was being selfish in looking at the matter from the perspective of "his time" instead of considering their son's love of soccer. Such different perceptions may be discussed amicably and conflicts resolved. Or they may be representative of many differences that will emerge with mounting resentment and a polarizing of attitudes. The same negative patterns that dissolved the marriage can poison the custody discussions.

Whether or not disagreement over money played a major role in the decision to divorce, money quickly becomes a divisive issue upon separation, especially if the marital home hasn't been sold. Maintaining two households obviously costs more than keeping one. In many cases one spouse will claim the other is using a custody battle to gain financial advantage. Often I have heard one parent assert that the other wouldn't pursue custody if money weren't the driving force. This may be true, because the amount of child support usually bears some relationship to the number of days per year a child lives with a parent. In some instances a spouse will continue to use money as a means of control. In more than one case an angry spouse has threatened to spend the other into poverty.

A stay-at-home mother may have to go back to work. If she has young children, she'll have to spend a lot of money for good, dependable child care. Working parents frequently encounter the dilemma of what to do when a child is ill. How sick is sick enough for a parent to miss work and stay home with the child?

After she separated from her husband, Joan resented Steven's forcing her into the job market when he was earning a very high salary. She believed that enrolling their emotionally disturbed son in a school after-care program or leaving him with a sitter was harmful. Joan was accustomed to being home so she could supervise her son while he completed his homework, after which she could structure his free time. As she saw it, Steven's insistence on her getting a job was mean-spirited and insensitive to the needs of their child.

For financial reasons a husband and wife may choose to separate by living in different parts of the marital home. The result is usually that the atmosphere becomes so emotionally charged that everyone spends as little time in the house as possible. In one family the tension got so unbearable that each parent left to stay with relatives during the other's time with the children. When separated adults reside in the home, nerves are so on edge that the slightest difference of opinion can trigger a fight.

One wife screamed at her husband for overstimulating their

daughter by reading Bible stories each night. One husband re-counted an argument flaring to the point that his wife hit, pushed, and spat at him, then locked him out. As he burst into the house after removing the lock with a screwdriver, she grabbed another screwdriver and rushed at him. The next day she petitioned the court for a restraining order to bar him from the property. In another family the parental interactions became so acrimonious that the maternal grandfather and paternal grandmother moved in to serve as peacekeepers. The grandparents slept at the house and alternated shifts preparing meals, maneuvering to avoid encounters with the battling parents.

If the parents live in different residences, there is far more to do than time allows—helping a child prepare for a special activity, transporting him to school, assembling his gear for a Scout camping trip, taking care of household repairs, and doing routine chores. Laundry piles up, groceries must be purchased, bills are due, the car has to be serviced. There is nothing remarkable about any of this, but for a single parent the burden seems staggering.

Many parents have said that their greatest anguish comes from dragging their child off to day care or to a sitter early in the morning and leaving her until late in the afternoon or early evening. Deborah's daughters were two and four. When she stayed at home the girls got up whenever they naturally awoke. Mornings mostly were unhurried as Deborah gave the children breakfast, picked out their clothes, dressed them, let them watch morning television shows for preschoolers as she did housework, then took them for an outing or to run errands. If either girl didn't feel well (both had allergies and respiratory difficulties), there was no pressure to go anywhere or do anything. After the separation Deborah had to return to work. What got to her was waking the children based on her schedule rather than their needs, rushing to dress and feed them, practically pushing them out the door into the car, then depositing them for nine hours at a day-care center. This was the routine, no matter how inclement the weather.

What mothers and fathers took for granted is no longer possible. Whatever dissension existed in the old household, usually two adults still managed to keep it operating. Groceries were in the refrigerator, the lawn was mowed, someone made sure the children had clean clothes and lunch money, and that they got to soccer practices and other activities. Perhaps one parent did most of what had to be done, but the other was available to pinch hit.

Divorcing parents have difficulty just making it through each day. The physical and emotional fatigue saps their enjoyment of life. They become anxious or depressed over the struggle to meet everyone's requirements. Some parents experience difficulty keeping up at their jobs. Divorce and custody litigation demands more of their time as they meet with lawyers, assemble personal papers, appear in court, and spend hours on other divorce-related matters. Something has to give because no parent can be on top of everything. At the end of a hectic day, an exhausted parent often finds that he has little left of himself to devote to his child.

Like a death, the demise of a marriage precipitates a grief reaction. In addition to feeling bereaved, you may feel less attractive, less likable, and generally less worthwhile. The race to be a superparent and do everything perfectly in order to disprove your spouse's allegations against you may leave you frantic, then exhausted and discouraged. Occasionally, you might even think those allegations aren't so far-fetched. Suffering from headaches, stomach upset, and lack of sleep, a mother castigated herself because she was irritable with her children. "Maybe I *am* this awful person," she remarked, referring to some of the deficiencies her husband continually cited.

Parents have told me how hard it is to abandon the hope of their child having a normal life. One father described his overwhelming sadness: "I'm like in a state of grief all the time. . . . I feel I'm uncontrollably crying. It hurts in my chest. It is like the death of a child. . . . I can't control when I get really teary. I sense my loss. My daughter won't have a normal life. You have a dream of how your relationship will be and the experience your child will have." This man stated that reminders of the death of his dream were "like getting your hand chopped off over and over."

Some parents experience an emotional collapse. The shock is greater when the marriage ends with little warning. After her husband left to pursue his relationship with another woman, Dianna turned to alcohol. On the way home from a restaurant, she was pulled over by a police officer and charged with driving under the influence. She found this experience "one heck of a wake-up call." In the aftermath of the arrest, Dianna berated herself for her weakness and resolved to abstain totally from alcoholic beverages. After months of sobriety she commented, "I still feel a tremendous amount of guilt. It was selfish. I wasn't taking into account the repercussions. I don't drink now. I don't even like to think about it." Discovering that she could manage on her own, not just as someone's wife, Dianna developed greater self-confidence. Still, it took nearly a year before she felt that she and her children had coalesced into "a real family."

During separation and divorce, second-guessing and fears persist. Parents may wonder whether the separation is precipitating problems worse than the marriage. A mother commented that she and her children were worse off in many respects. The family had lived in a spacious, comfortable colonial house. Now she and her two sons were crammed into a one-bedroom apartment. Before the separation she spent far more time with her sons. Now she had to work longer hours, leave the children in day care, and didn't see them at all on the days they spent with their father.

I have talked to parents whose plummeting self-confidence affected areas of their lives in which they had always been successful. They became less productive at work and wondered how long they could continue to merit their employers' confidence. One father told me that his supervisor would be stunned to know what an emotional wreck he was. He feared that fatigue and depression would eventually cost him his job, the only part of his life he felt good about.

Friends and neighbors knew each parent as part of a couple. Finding it difficult to stay on an even footing with both husband and wife after the separation, some withdraw totally; others befriend one and drop the other. The falling away of long-term relationships also diminishes parental self-confidence.

Some parents, desiring to prove to themselves that they still are attractive, plunge into dating and making sexual conquests. Some are so emotionally needy that they quickly become intimate, then are devastated when relationships don't work out. If they aren't legally divorced, a new relationship can damage their custody case, especially if the children are drawn into their involvement with another person.

All this is bad enough for adults. Now consider it from your child's point of view.

Chapter 2

The Child's Experience: Loss After Loss

Parental separation marks the end of family life as your child has known it. No matter what problems you and your spouse have had, you've been your child's anchor. As your marriage disintegrates, your child's world falls apart. After parents separate, no matter which parent the child is with, someone is always missing. Most boys and girls I have interviewed expressed a deep sadness similar to mourning after a death.*

Long before you decided to separate, your child felt sad and angry as he witnessed parental discord in its many forms. Worse than the bickering and yelling loomed the prospect that Mom and Dad might not stay together. Nine-year-old Eric told me his parents argued every week and his dad was pushing his mom around. He was really upset because his dad said that his mom couldn't go with him and his sister to Disney World. "My mom says she doesn't want to

---

* In her longitudinal study of children of divorce, Judith Wallerstein observed that the negative aftermath never ends. "Divorce is a cumulative experience. Its impact increases over time and rises to a crescendo in adulthood. . . . It's in adulthood that children of divorce suffer most." J. S. Wallerstein et al., *The Unexpected Legacy of Divorce* (New York: Hyperion, 2000), pp. 298–299.

go where she's not wanted," Eric said. Then he added, "I told her she's wanted by me." He confided that he worried about his parents getting divorced. When I asked which would be worse, for things to stay as they were, with his parents not getting along and yelling at each other, or for his parents to get a divorce, Eric responded without hesitation that a divorce would be far worse. "I want them to be together," he stated emphatically, as do most kids I talk with. Asked if he could wish for anything in the world that he would like, Eric stated, "To have no more arguments, for my mom and dad to be nice to each other."

When you're divorcing, it's easy to lose sight of a very basic fact: Your child has been used to seeing the two of you together almost every day of his or her life—your togetherness is as much a given as the existence of day and night. Although seven-year-old Todd was relieved that his separated parents no longer fought, he stated, "I don't get to see them all the time—I can't see them together." He would be with his mom *or* his dad. But never again could he spend time with both of them together. Although this is obvious to adults, it is often overlooked as a source of anguish for a child.

To many children divorce just does not make sense. Max believed that, despite all the strife, his parents still loved each other. He explained to me, "When my sister's mad at my mom, my mom still says she loves her." He thought the same must be true of his parents. Even though he knew divorce was possible, he refused to accept that it would happen in his family. I asked six-year-old Emily why her parents weren't living together anymore. She replied, "I know why. They keep arguing and shouting bad words like 'shut up.' That's a bad word to say. I know they don't care about each other anymore. I know it doesn't make sense. It never will make sense to me."

Even children who lived in truly terrible conditions desperately want the family reunited. If they didn't want everyone living together, these children sought assurance that both parents would remain involved with them. I interviewed a seven-year-old girl whose father was in prison for sexually molesting her. Although more than a year had passed since he was sentenced, she persistently questioned her mother about when her daddy could come home to live with them. In idealizing what family life had been and fantasizing what it would be, she seemed not to consider what her father had done to her. Eight-year-old Ted said that his father was mean to both him and his mother. I found Ted's dad irate and embittered, and so did a judge, who put him in jail for contempt of court. Nevertheless, when I asked Ted what three things he wished for, number one was that "my poppa and mom live together again."

Barbara's parents had joint custody of her and lived just fifteen minutes apart. Although this eleven-year-old disclosed that her stepfather had spanked, kicked, and punched her, she was far more disturbed about her biological father's filing a lawsuit to make her live with him. Barbara commented, "I don't really care just as long as I get to see my mom and my dad." She explained, "Some days, I get real mad and want to live at Dad's. When I go to Dad's and get mad, I want to live at Mom's."

Sometimes a youngster will not actually say he wants his parents to reconcile, but he may express indirectly how he feels during a psychological evaluation. A psychologist described thirteen-year-old Raymond's responses to testing, which left no doubt regarding his emotional state:

More like a much younger child, he drew himself touching and holding hands with both parental figures. . . . On [one item Raymond] was asked to choose a barn ("Mom" barn or "Dad" barn) for a horse to return to after a tiring day. Not only did he choose to have the horse return to both, but the strain he is feeling caught between his battling parents is captured in the pictorial manner in which he portrays the pulling and splitting the horse is experiencing.

It isn't that children forget the unhappy moments during all the parental rancor, but their idealization of family life overshadows their memory of the grimmer realities. Even after a parent remarries, a child's fantasy of the family living together under one roof may endure.

Having lost the family as a unit, children are apprehensive about the future. Nine-year-old Alex said that he was worried "about my mom and my dad—like what's gonna happen." His wish was "that we could have a nice family and that I'd get to see them more often and they'd live in the same house." The child's fear is heightened if she thinks she may lose contact with a parent. This is particularly so when she perceives one parent engaged in maneuvers to remove the other from her life. A colleague I consulted in such a case described a seven-year-old girl's view of life as extremely precarious: "According to the portrait she paints, the world is poorly controlled, vaguely dangerous, and seems to be changing in negative and ever more threatening ways."

Some youngsters feel they have lost any semblance of control over their lives. First, they weren't consulted about the family breakup. Then they find themselves swept along in the maelstrom of their parents' custody battle. Again, they feel they have little or no say about what will happen to them. A ten-year-old girl was having difficulty absorbing her parents' deteriorating relationship. In a perplexed manner she stated, "They won't speak to each other at all; they used to love talking to each other." Sensing she had no control over the future, she said with resignation, "Whoever wins I stay with."

A school counselor described a youngster in her divorce group as "feeling like a human guinea pig." She commented, "He wishes he could go back to being a kid." A twelve-year-old boy angrily asserted, "It seems like my sister and I are being treated like possessions— argued over like a chair. A chair can't think. We should be able to decide what we want to do. I'm sick of being told that there are some things I don't understand. . . . I'd rather be told them and not understand than not be told them at all." Feeling like a Ping-Pong ball, this youngster was fed up and stated, "I'm ready to get on with my life." With parental conflict continuing to swirl around them, these children feel stuck.

Their fear and sense of powerlessness are heightened when children witness scenes in which their parents are at each other's throats. Nine-year-old Trevor told me of an upsetting situation that had just occurred: "Mom got in the car. She didn't want to leave us. Then Dad tried to pull her out of the car. . . . He stopped because we cried and cried. We didn't know what to do. We were scared, I mean really scared! I didn't know what to say. We just cried." Shortly after Trevor related this event, I asked him what he would choose to be if he could be any animal. In his answer he expressed both his vulnerability and his desire to be tough. "I want to be a wolf. People shoot 'em. I'm not a wolf. I want to be a bird . . . because they can fly up to the clouds. Some die, but I'm a tough bird—an eagle, they're better than other birds; they're strong."

Children want to feel that their parents are listening to them. Although they would like to have some control over their lives, they don't want the responsibility of deciding where they will live. They freeze emotionally at the prospect of having to choose one parent over the other because they believe they must be fair to both. By stating a preference, they risk hurting a parent's feelings and losing his or her affection. Some are apprehensive that, by even hinting at a preference for one parent, they will appear disloyal to the other.

During evaluations I sometimes ask a child whom he would take to live with him on a desert island if he could bring only one person.* (First, I ascertain whether he knows what a desert island is.) Some children quickly name either one or the other parent. However, there is generally considerable hesitation as they ponder their answers. Some boys and girls quickly figure out what this question is getting at and find a way to avoid naming a parent. Eight-year-old Angie told me that she would take her sister. Asked why, she explained, "Because if I took my mom, it wouldn't be fair to my dad, and if I took my dad, it wouldn't be fair to my mom. And I don't have two sisters. So it'd be fair if I took my sister."

Some children, like seven-year-old Wendy, are so apprehensive about appearing to favor one parent over the other that they won't disclose even basic information about their mom and dad. Hurt and angry about her parents separating, Wendy found it much less

---

* The "island game" is described as a technique for child custody evaluations in D. Skafte, *Child Custody Evaluations: A Practical Guide* (Beverly Hills: Sage Publications, 1985), pp. 106–107.

threatening to complain about her older sister teasing and calling her names. Asked if either parent said mean things about the other, Wendy replied that both did. Asked who put her to bed at night when the family was together, she stated, "I go to bed by myself." Asked whether anyone comes to her room to say good night, she said, "Both, not at the same time." When I asked her to draw a picture of her family, it took her fifteen minutes to complete the task. The finished picture showed all four family members—both parents, Wendy, and her sister—together.

Wendy continued her evenhanded answers to all questions about her mom and dad, even in the most mundane aspects of life. Asked who reminds her to brush her teeth, she replied, "When my dad's there, my dad does. When Mom is there, Mom does." Both parents were taking her to church, although each to a different church. Asked whether she liked one church better than the other, she said, "I like them both the same."

Responding to the desert island question, Wendy said she would take her girlfriend and neighbor. Asked if she could take one person from her family, she quickly named her sister. When I pushed a little further and said that she could take another family member with whom she would live, she specified the dog. Wendy's precarious stance was reflected in her response to being asked to draw a house, a tree, and a person.★ The person was way up in the air, perhaps indicating how she felt during the continuing deterioration of family relationships.

★ Through these three drawings, a person may indirectly reveal aspects of his personality. See "House-Tree-Person Projective Drawing Technique (H-T-P)" (Los Angeles: Western Psychological Services).

Some children appear to have accepted the family breakup. Not only do they seem resigned to it but they may also express relief that they no longer have to hear constant arguing or witness the abusive interactions of their parents. But within there still lingers a sense of loss and profound sadness. Preschoolers may show their distress by becoming withdrawn. Some revert to sucking their thumbs, rocking, wetting the bed, soiling themselves, or engaging in other behavior more typical of a younger age.

Many children of divorcing parents wonder whether they did something to cause the breakup. Like many children, they have overheard their parents arguing about them. Trying to understand why their parents no longer want to live together, these youngsters conjecture that if they had behaved better this wouldn't be happening. It's not unusual to find a child acting like a negotiator or peacemaker. Having functioned in this capacity before the separation, he continues to think he can patch up the damage and even promote reconciliation.

A well-known book on divorce sets forth the premise that children of divorce can have "two happy homes."* Put yourself in the place of the child. How would you feel about shuttling back and forth between your parents' homes, dividing your time, your possessions, your loyalty, and your love? I have yet to meet a child who didn't have problems with this. Children grow accustomed to all sorts of situations. They make necessary adjustments. However, their apparent resilience doesn't mean that they're happy about living at two homes rather than with their entire family in one.

* Isolina Ricci, *Mom's House, Dad's House* (New York: Fireside, 1997).

When a child's parents separate, his or her life becomes more complicated. Usually parents aren't sufficiently well off financially for a child to have two complete sets of possessions, including a full wardrobe, computer, stereo, bicycle, athletic equipment, games, and toys. Back and forth, boys and girls carry backpacks crammed with schoolbooks and assignments. They start a school project at one house, then cart it to the other to work on it.

Imagine being ready to drive your child to a softball game only to discover that the uniform is at your spouse's home and he's out of town. Calendars must be coordinated so that children don't miss sports practices and games, birthday parties, and other events. Take your child's own birthday party, something he or she usually anticipates with excitement. Now it may be fraught with tension. Does your child have two parties, one at each home? Do you invite the same friends to both, or different people to each? What do you do if your child wants you to invite the other parent?

Your child may have to give up participating in activities he once enjoyed. Much to his dismay, Tony could play for his soccer team only when he was spending time with his father, since his mother's work schedule made it difficult to transport him to games. When Tony spent weekends with her, she wanted to do things with him, not sit in the bleachers. The coach allowed Tony to participate when he could. But, missing half the practices, Tony became self-conscious. The coach told me that he was astonished to see Tony go out of his way to avoid the ball so he wouldn't risk making a mistake. Although he was a good athlete, Tony seemed intimidated by his team members, who practiced together regularly. Finally, Tony felt so inferior to the other boys he quit a sport that once had been his passion.

In the aftermath of the separation, your standard of living may drop. You and your child may have to forgo extras, such as vacations or eating out. If the family home is sold, a move may be necessary to less spacious or comfortable quarters, possibly in a neighborhood that isn't as good and where the schools are of a lower caliber. Your child may have to drop out of extracurricular activities or lessons because you can no longer afford equipment, uniforms, or travel. Your child may lose a nanny or other household employee to whom he or she is attached because neither you nor your spouse can handle the expense alone.

The issue isn't that a child is deprived because he cannot have a nanny, designer clothes, or trips to resorts. It is the change that is stressful, and parental separation usually requires a child to make many major changes simultaneously. He may lose nearly everything that is familiar. If he has to move to a new neighborhood, he no longer has his community of friends and classmates, who could offer support. To nine-year-old Norma, the prospect of moving was terrifying. Stating that she is shy and has trouble making friends, she was practically in a panic about leaving her classmates and neighborhood playmates.

Some youngsters grow accustomed to moving, especially if their parents serve in the military, foreign service, or other occupations that require changes in assignment. However, their families usually remain intact. Moving when the secure foundation of the family unit is breaking apart is more difficult.

Perhaps the greatest loss for a child is spending less time with either or both parents and more time in the company of sitters or other providers of day care. There is loss of leisure on weekends as well. A separated working mother or father may spend Saturday taking a child along to grocery shop, pick up a prescription, stop at the cleaner's, and run other errands that couldn't be done on week-days. On Sundays, hours are spent cleaning, mowing the lawn, doing laundry.

Another sort of loss—one that young children don't compre-hend—occurs when a close relationship with a grandparent or other relative is disrupted. Seven-year-old Barry was very close to his paternal grandparents and had regarded their home as a refuge from his parents' strife. But Barry's mother had long disliked her in-laws because she thought that, in spoiling her son, they were undermin-ing her. Mild resentment boiled into hatred when her in-laws finan-cially and emotionally supported her husband in his custody suit. So convinced was she that the grandparents would try to turn her son against her that Barry's mother refused even to consider resolving custody issues out of court unless the final agreement included a provision that her in-laws could not spend time with Barry unless his father was present.

Your child may also be affected in unanticipated ways as both parents' relationships with neighbors and family friends change. During a holiday party a girl overheard one neighbor tell another about seeing her mother in the company of a man who was not her father. The child was crushed by what she heard and mortified to have it come out of the mouth of the mother of one of her best friends. She felt betrayed by this woman, who had been like a sec-ond mother to her.

As you and your spouse rebuild your lives, your child may ex-perience loss after loss. Children whose parents are separating may find themselves having to adjust to disruptive, arbitrary, or nonsensi-cal arrangements.

Telephone contact is an example of a battleground in which a child may continually find himself in the path of his parents' vendettas against each other. A parent may refuse to answer and instruct the child not to answer the phone if caller ID reveals that the other parent is on the line. I have heard parents accuse each other of deactivating the answering machine, failing to give the child a message, or refusing to allow a child to return a call. Sometimes these charges are true; sometimes they are concocted to make the other parent look bad. A parent may erroneously conclude that his child has been prevented from talking to him when in fact the youngster was in the middle of an activity he did not want to interrupt. I have known parents to insist that, no matter what their child is doing, the other parent must put the child on the phone.

At one extreme is the parent who rarely calls because she doesn't want to get embroiled with the other. The child may not understand why his mother or father doesn't call. Other parents believe that their child must hear their voice every night and insist on calling even though they have little to say and don't consider what they may interrupt. One three-year-old was so irritated by her father's frequent calling that she told him, "You're not my father." The enraged father called his attorney, complaining that his ex-wife was poisoning the child against him.

Sometimes parents are so unwilling to cooperate that the court establishes a designated hour for calls. Then everyone becomes a prisoner to the specified time. I have known traveling parents to pull off the highway to place a long-distance call just to ensure that they are complying with the court order.

Some children in the center of a custody battle suffer a profound loss that they may never fully articulate. They learned that marriage is a wonderful, worthy goal: People fall in love, marry, have children. But that perspective is shattered as they witness the opposite occur with their own parents. One boy, whose parents had fought over him from the time he was nine until he was fourteen, had no hope that their wrangling would subside. He declared that he wanted no part of marriage and having children. It was as though he felt he was destined to divorce and have his children suffer the same fate as he.

> If this [a divorce and custody battle] happened, I know what they would feel like. If I get divorced, I know this whole thing will start over in a new generation of families. Practically all my friends are living with their mom or their dad. It's kind of sad. People can't get along anymore. When you see Grandma or Grandpa, they can't all be there. The [parents] would both be fighting. You have to throw two birthday parties for them just to get their families in. And Christmas, Thanksgiving, and Easter, you know . . . I don't know.

This is just an overview of the many losses children experience as their parents go through a divorce. In part IV I'll identify specific errors that parents make, compounding the suffering of their offspring. Then I'll recommend specific steps you can take to help your child cope with this very difficult time of life.

II

Parents' Personalities

Your LIFELONG PATTERN of dealing with conflict determines how you will cope with marital separation and divorce. Above all else, the critical factor in resolving child custody disputes is the personalities of the parents. The divorcing couples I interview generally fall into three categories: problem solvers, controllers, and the impaired. These aren't formal psychiatric or psychological diagnoses but personality types. Into which category do you fall?

Chapter 3

Problem Solvers, Controllers, and the Impaired

PROBLEM SOLVERS STRIVE to work through crises constructively. Controllers perceive other people as pawns to be maneuvered
for their own gain. These individuals regard control as an end in itself. The impaired are so emotionally disabled that they don't cooperate with problem solvers because they fail to approach situations
rationally. They are so needy and vulnerable that they fall prey to
controllers. Impaired spouses may be depressed, in denial, addicted
to alcohol or drugs, or they may have a psychiatric diagnosis.

I use these terms to describe what lawyers, psychologists, and
others observe when they watch parents resolve or magnify their differences over the custody of their children. The following summa-
rizes patterns of interaction among parents in these three categories
as they approach child custody.

Problem Solver Married to a Problem Solver

Both parents work to minimize conflict and constructively address problems. They're not out to achieve a victory or seek revenge. These parents are thoughtful and practical as they strive to settle upon an arrangement they truly hope will serve the best interest of their child.

Problem Solver Married to a Controller

While one spouse genuinely desires to resolve conflicts, the controller is uncompromising. The controller's usually unstated agenda involves winning custody mainly to frustrate the other spouse.

Problem Solver Married to an Impaired Parent

The problem solver must determine the best way to interact with a parent who is unable to assume custodial responsibility because of an emotional or psychiatric disability or addiction. If, as is often the case, the other parent does not consider himself or herself impaired, that parent frustrates the problem solver's efforts to work toward effective solutions.

Controller Married to a Controller

Each spouse tries to prevail in struggles over even the most inconsequential matters. Each deploys a barrage of tactics to dominate or destroy the other. While avowing that they are acting on behalf of their child, they are instead extremely self-absorbed.

Controller Married to an Impaired Parent

The controller capitalizes on any perceived weakness of the impaired parent. Before a court determines custody, the controller may have taken over decision making and care of the child, neither of which may be to the child's benefit.

Impaired Parent Married to an Impaired Parent

Both parents are so consumed by fear, depression, addiction, or whatever else that they need outside guidance to establish a stable environment for their child. Social services, mental health professionals, or a special lawyer for the child (known as a guardian ad litem) may become involved during custody litigation.

Two Problem Solvers

Disappointment, depression, anxiety, and anger are all common emotions experienced by divorcing parents. The challenge is for mothers and fathers to deal constructively with these emotions and establish a new independent life that offers them and their child stability and opportunity. Problem solvers do this rather than fuel vendettas and seek revenge. They aim to resolve conflicts rather than create new ones.

These parents love their child more than they dislike each other. They usually give the highest priority to what is best for their son or daughter. These individuals have been problem solvers in other areas of life, willing to work hard, compromise, and negotiate. They are accustomed to looking at issues from the point of view of others rather than simply imposing their own will. They have been empathic with their child. Even as their marriage disintegrated, they tried to shield their child from conflict. When it became clear that they would have to separate, they talked to their child about it and remained supportive. Recognizing when they needed support, these parents were not averse to seeking professional help.

In the midst of turmoil, problem solvers think about how to protect their offspring. These mothers and fathers recognize that their child needs both parents—that the loss of the family unit shouldn't be compounded by loss of access to either of them. These parents regard each other as equals. They work things out without involving the child, ensuring that he or she doesn't feel pressured to choose between the parents. Problem solvers remain flexible regarding day-to-day arrangements and avoid squabbling over "my time" versus "your time." They share information and cooperate in decision making. If they reach an impasse, they are amenable to mediation by a third party.

Some courts require that divorcing parents first try to mediate their differences. Writing in *The Matrimonial Strategist,* Mary Kay Kisthardt and Barbara Ellen Handschu discuss the rationale behind having parents engage in mediation before litigation: "Bringing parents together and encouraging them to resolve jointly problems involving their children will, it is hoped, set the stage for future cooperation, which, in turn, ultimately will benefit the children."* The authors point out that whether mediation is a viable approach

---

* M. K. Kisthardt and B. E. Handschu, "Facilitating Negotiation of Child Custody or Visitation Disputes Through Mediation," *Matrimonial Strategist,* vol. 10 (April 2000), p. 1.

depends upon whether a client thinks he or she can "effectively and fairly work with the other parent and not be intimidated by, or fearful of, the interaction." In my terminology here, mediation is most likely to be successful when engaged in by two problem solvers. A positive outcome is less likely if there is an imbalance of power or if one or both parents are impaired.

In some situations—unfortunately, not usually those I encounter in my practice—parents work out their differences by themselves. They want to save time and money, and they believe that they can co-parent their child despite all that has soured them on each other.

Sue and Tony had abandoned any hope of reconciling their marriage. On their own they drew up papers dividing what little property they had and stipulating they would have joint custody of their six-year-old son and three-year-old daughter. Both Sue and Tony thought it best for the children to live with their mother until adolescence, at which time they would reevaluate. Both parents continued to live in the same small town and remained cordial. They had few problems making decisions and sharing information. Several years later Sue remarried and started to have marital difficulties. She and Tony agreed that the children should live with him, and the transition occurred smoothly.

This situation was never litigated. In fact, neither parent hired an attorney. When the couple appeared in court and presented the document they had prepared, the judge granted the divorce and endorsed the custody arrangement. I heard about the case through meeting one of the parents. With all the discord I have seen, it was reassuring to hear about two parents quietly and cooperatively resolving differences in a manner beneficial to their children.

When problem solvers reach an impasse, they are still inclined to work things out rather than fight. Stuart and Linda consulted me after failing to reach an agreement through mediation over the schedule for sharing time with their infant son. The mediator cautioned them in a letter:

> I am writing to you both because it is clear that your situation is tottering on the brink of becoming adversarial, with all of the expense, time, and frustration of that process. . . . I cannot fault your respective positions. . . . You both care very deeply about [your son] and I have the sense that you are both excellent parents. . . . The worst case scenario for [your son's] development would be that one of you gets relegated to being a secondary parent after a bitter, expensive, and time-consuming process.

In a note to me articulating what he desired to accomplish, Stuart emphasized that, for their child's sake, he had not abandoned hope that he and his wife could reach an agreement. Linda expressed the same sentiment. She confided that she understood she still had a lot of anger and feared that unresolved personal matters were interfering with her doing what was best. She added, "I believe both parents should be involved in decision making." Clearly, she and Stuart concurred on this most important matter and were willing to work together.

Linda and Stuart had already agreed in principle to a 50-50 time split, but they squabbled over its implementation. Whereas Linda was professing to favor what she termed "maximum exposure to both parents," she thought their son rightfully should spend more time with her simply because she was the mother. Although they came close to going to court, Linda and Stuart overcame their animosity and possessiveness, and worked out a mutually satisfactory schedule for sharing custody. They realized that whether the time division was 55-45 or 52-48 was less important than building a cooperative relationship, remaining flexible, and enjoying their son.

A Problem Solver and a Controller

Many marriages break up when a noncontrolling husband or wife stands up to a controller. By refusing to endure any longer the mistreatment dished out for years, the noncontrolling spouse precipitates a crisis. The marriage may have gone smoothly in the controller's opinion, largely because he or she went unchallenged. In reality, though, the noncontroller had walked a tightrope. As a problem solver, he or she has sought to avoid unnecessary and debilitating conflict and picked battles discerningly. Having the welfare of the child uppermost in his or her thoughts, the problem-solving parent let a lot go by rather than subject the household to unpleasantness. When he or she finally becomes fed up with walking on eggshells and decides to do something, the marital equilibrium is disrupted. The noncontrolling spouse's sudden assertiveness strikes at the core of the controller's self-concept. At home he or she has been accustomed to having his or her way. Now things are different. The controller reacts by angrily faulting the other spouse for creating the upheaval. If the problem solver fails to back down, the controller becomes more irascible and domineering.

In truth, the controller is an abuser. When family members get out of line, he or she becomes harsh and punitive. In extreme cases spouse and offspring know that at any time they may be berated, threatened, or even physically attacked. I have seen a controller psychologically grind down his spouse so severely that she had to seek medical treatment and was placed on tranquilizers or antidepressants. Then the controller alleged that her taking medication confirmed what he'd asserted all along, that she was a disturbed person and an unfit parent. Were he to be asked about his contribution to the marital difficulties, he would portray himself as the victim who had to endure the erratic moods and capricious demands of his unstable partner.

While creating a living hell in the family, the controller may appear to others as a generous individual and a proponent of a strong family. Gregarious and charming, he or she enlists the support and sympathy of neighbors, friends, and even relatives who have not had to live with him or her.

During the separation and divorce proceedings, the controller is determined to maintain the upper hand. Now the problem solver is the enemy! The controller is a formidable adversary as he or she enters the legal arena to fight for child custody. Whereas the problem-solving spouse wants to resolve differences, the controller is intent on revenge and winning. The spouse desperately wants to reach a settlement and move on with life, but the controller's notion of a settlement is for the problem solver to agree to his or her conditions. If he or she doesn't capitulate, the controller will react angrily and become intent upon destroying the spouse, even threatening financial ruin or tarnishing of reputation. Of course, the most dire threat is to take away what the spouse values most—the child. Whether or not these intentions are verbalized, the controller's spouse knows what he or she is capable of. The problem solver is also well aware of the controller's success at charming others and convincing them of the correctness of his or her position. I have had men and women warn me about this as I began a custody evaluation. They worry that I won't be able to penetrate their spouse's persuasive front. Even more, they fear that a judge might be taken in.

The controller's attorney is likely to regard the new client as a conscientious, devoted parent who has been unjustly maligned by the other spouse. Initially the controller is eager to collaborate with his or her attorney and relishes mapping out a battle plan. However, if he or she senses that the litigation is not going as planned, the affability fades, and the controller becomes harder to deal with. I have known controllers to fire their attorneys, refuse to pay them, or threaten to sue them for malpractice.

If the controller participates in a custody evaluation, get ready for something approaching a game of chess. He or she cases out the evaluator to determine what that person wants to hear and needs to know. One reason a custody evaluation may take weeks or even months is that personalities reveal themselves slowly. Eventually, though, the patient evaluator will penetrate the controller's facade.

Wanting to avoid a confrontation, particularly one that might unfairly involve the child, the problem solver tries to remain reasonable and flexible. The controller perceives any form of accommodation as an indicator of weakness and becomes even more intransigent. Aware that he or she is losing ground, the problem solver may be forced to enter the fray. The stakes can hardly be higher. With the assistance of his or her legal counsel and perhaps a personal therapist, and the encouragement of friends and relatives, the problem solver may finally stand up to his or her spouse.

This was the case with Sandra, who managed to extricate herself from her marriage to Bruce, in which she had felt trapped for years.

Bruce and Sandra seemed to have the ideal marriage. Sandra told me, "You put on a happy face to the outside world. Some people just see your happy face." With Bruce earning more than $100,000, Sandra had been able to stay home to raise their three children. The marriage had gone along for fourteen years with only a few ripples of discord because Sandra was enjoying doing what she had dreamed about since she was a little girl, being a full-time wife and mother. Once her children were spending six hours a day in school, Sandra had more time to herself, and she started thinking about developing a part-time career. She said nothing about this to Bruce. It was often this way. A lot of things Sandra considered, she eventually dismissed because she didn't want to upset Bruce. Although increasingly dissatisfied with her life, Sandra remained silent but, she said, with "a piece of myself slowly dying. I realized how I've been manipulated for years," she told me. "I have no power, no voice in our relationship. He's led me to feel I'm not a partner."

What brought matters to a head was her beginning to work part-time at a sales job. Although Sandra worked from home, occasionally she would attend an evening meeting and, once in a while, travel to a convention. Bruce did not take well to this because he was accustomed to having Sandra at his beck and call. Sandra tried to discuss her work with her husband, but his response was to ridicule her, demean her employer, and badger her about neglecting the family. Sadly, she recalled, "I was trying to get his understanding and support. How could someone make me feel so small and insignificant?" Then Bruce accused her of having an affair with a colleague. Dismayed and incredulous, Sandra told me that he had become truly desperate to concoct such a story.

One night Sandra did not come home when Bruce expected. He started dialing hospitals and then called the police. When his wife entered the house with apologies for being late, he berated her about being with another man. Actually she had been out to dinner with six people from her company. Sandra reported that her husband ranted until the early hours of the morning, becoming so hysterical that he demanded to know where his gun was. This was a firearm Bruce had insisted upon buying and keeping in the house over his wife's vociferous objection, especially since she feared their three children might come upon it. The next morning she found the gun, entrusted it to a relative for safekeeping, and consulted an attorney. Although she was unnerved by Bruce's behavior, Sandra was even more distraught over her attorney's recommendation to leave her home immediately with the children. She did not heed his advice, and the situation worsened dramatically.

Finally Bruce got fed up, informed Sandra the house was his, and demanded that she leave. In another altercation Bruce slapped Sandra across the face and declared, "We're at war now." Only then did she take the children and stay with friends. In response, Bruce changed the locks on the doors and closed the credit card accounts.

By the time Sandra came to me during the custody evaluation, she could hardly believe that her life had changed so drastically. From happily tucking the children into bed in the family's half-million-dollar colonial, she had become, as she put it, "an alien in my own house." Now a single mother, she was locked in combat with the man with whom she had expected to spend her life. Sandra told me that her every move was "under a microscope" as Bruce tried to prove her an unfit mother. "He's so mad at me that I crumbled his little world. He wants to hurt me. He wants to financially devastate me and take the children away."

As Bruce became nastier, Sandra feared he would turn the children against her. "The kids perceive Daddy in a big house, getting a new car, joining the country club, and I'm buying mattresses. They ask, 'Mommy, are you poor now?' It's very scary. . . . Every time he has them, he's telling them things. They came to me and said, 'Mommy, why are you forcing Daddy to sell the house?' Is there a way to make him stop?"

Defending herself was difficult. Sandra recoiled from telling the children their father was a liar. To denigrate Bruce would be to put the children in the middle. Bruce had their daughter so convinced that Sandra was having an affair that the child leafed through her mom's telephone book and quizzed her about names. The daughter's therapist stated that she was "a real depressed kid, inundated by information which she shouldn't have." The therapist thought both parents were at fault but believed that Bruce was more the instigator while Sandra was reacting in self-defense.

Because she was established in her own home and had the children living with her, Bruce intensified his efforts to control Sandra's life. No matter what the issue, he imposed one condition after another. He warned that in order to get her support check on time, Sandra had to meet him at a specific place and time. When she picked up the children for a holiday outing, Bruce thrust papers at her and demanded she sign them before he'd release the children.

I saw that the three children had strong bonds with both parents. No clear preference for either emerged. Although Bruce bullied his wife, he was loving toward his children. He was very involved in their schooling, athletic programs, and other interests. Nearly everyone I interviewed said that Bruce was a devoted father. I recommended a joint custody arrangement in which the children would live primarily with their mother. Bruce would spend a lot of weekends, holidays, and summer vacation time with them. Although he believed that I should have reversed the arrangement, Bruce decided it would be fruitless to go to court and risk losing. After months of combat, legal fees exceeding $50,000, and emotional exhaustion, the couple hammered out a custody agreement. But long after the consent agreement was filed with the court, Bruce continued to try to push Sandra around.

In cases like this, further struggles always lie around the corner. If something, such as a new relationship, distracts the controller, the other parent may have a reprieve. The controller may tone down his attempts to dominate his ex-spouse if he or she remarries and has a new arena in which to exercise control. But invariably new issues arise, and the controller remains determined to prevail.

A Problem Solver and an Impaired Parent

In child custody cases all sorts of deficiencies and conditions are alleged. Spouses call each other alcoholics and level many other charges. When the smoke clears, most of these allegations are revealed as either false or gross exaggerations. A spouse might be mildly and temporarily unable to function at 100 percent, but that doesn't render him or her incompetent to care for a child. In speaking of an impaired parent, I am referring to a chronic condition that interferes with a man's or woman's ability to function as a responsible, custodial parent. The impairment may be a disabling mental illness, chronic misuse of mind-altering substances, severe emotional volatility, or an abusive parenting style. A person may be so dependent that he will not let go of his spouse emotionally. Professing to detest his ex-spouse, the dependent parent may perpetuate all sorts of conflicts to maintain contact.

The most obvious case of psychological impairment, although it does not in and of itself render a parent unfit, is a psychotic condition in which the person is out of touch with reality. A mother of two children told me that she was the Virgin Mary and her son was Jesus Christ. Suffering from a number of delusions and enormous anxiety, she agreed to be hospitalized. The difficulties regarding custody emerged after her discharge. Her husband sued for exclusive use of the marital home and temporary sole custody. He also asked that his wife be supervised when spending time with their son because she was still behaving erratically. Convinced that the child's safety was paramount, the judge ordered that mother and son spend time together only with a supervisor present, at least until her psychological condition could be more fully assessed.

The impaired parent is likely to deny that a problem exists, even in instances of a clearly documented psychotic disorder. The psychotic mother I just described saw no reason to move out of her home and believed that she was totally fit to take care of her son. Whatever the evidence of impairment, the parent offers excuses, blames other people, and minimizes the significance of the behavior in question. He perceives nothing about his conduct as potentially disadvantageous to the child. His defense is to launch an offensive, which is likely to entail dragging the other parent and the child through a lengthy ordeal over custody.

Frank was a father who believed he was helping his children when he was actually mistreating them. His mother described him as "a loving but very strict" parent. "Very strict" turned out to be a massive understatement. Frank imposed severe discipline to beat religious teachings into his children. He told me, "A lot of my ideas are from Christian books." Believing literally in "spare the rod and spoil the child," he used a three-foot-long curtain rod with a steel tip to deliver a memorable sting. He explained that he had read "not to use your hand, but the instrument is to be feared." He said that he kept the rods handy but used them infrequently. One time he struck his younger son because he got out of bed when he wasn't supposed to. Frank considered the mere threat of using the rods a powerful deterrent to misbehavior because "they look pretty scary." He commented, "I had a motto: The whinies get it on the heinies."

A lifeguard told me that Frank took his son into a rest room at the swimming pool and spanked him repeatedly with his hand, then pinched his mouth shut so he couldn't cry. On another occasion Frank was seen grabbing a Ping-Pong paddle and striking his nine-year-old son on the back. The boy told me his father had kicked him, struck him with the curtain rod, hit him "with a stick with little things on it," spanked him with a twig, washed his mouth out with soap, grabbed him and squeezed his arm, and spanked him innumerable times with his hand. Yet nothing that I heard from anyone I interviewed suggested that this boy was especially difficult to manage. His teacher rated him "satisfactory" in accepting responsibility, "good" with regard to courteous behavior, and "good" about listening and following directions.

Frank hadn't always been so religious. He acknowledged that he had been a heavy drinker and would "become cranky if I didn't have my beer." He also revealed that before his marriage he had been involved in a homosexual relationship. Turning to religion was his attempt to combat his sexual impulses, which were at odds with his idealized concept of a husband and father. After his baptism Frank shattered his rock and roll records and listened only to religious programming and music. Because he saw the secular world as filled with evil, he isolated his children. They weren't allowed to bring friends home from school, nor could they play at other kids' homes. Their social life was restricted to associating with boys and girls from Sunday school and church, none of whom were invited to the house.

Frank staunchly defended his views and child-rearing practices. He regarded his wife as an infidel who undermined him by creating a laissez-faire and immoral atmosphere for their sons. I didn't agree with his characterization of his spouse. Rather, I saw her as struggling to cope with her husband's tyrannical regimen. Trying to compensate for her husband's harshness, she was somewhat permissive although still very attentive and responsible.

In my custody report I wrote that Frank had "been so restrictive of his children that they have in fact been in danger of losing precious parts of their childhood and important opportunities for socialization." I recommended that the two boys live with their mother and spend time with their father only under the supervision of a relative whom I knew to be more moderate and responsible. I also recommended that Frank receive psychotherapy and instruction in parenting skills and suggested a review after Frank had been in therapy for six months and completed the parenting course. This was to give him hope that he might have more contact with his children. Hurt and angry, Frank seemed determined to oppose my recommendations in court. His attorney listened to him ventilate, expressed his sympathy, then convinced Frank not to go to court because any judge hearing the case would regard his disciplinary measures as abusive and order similar restrictions.

There was no doubt that Frank loved his children, and they loved him in return, despite his harshness. Yet this father was so impaired that he could rarely look at any situation from a child's viewpoint. He showed almost no tolerance for his sons' mistakes but came down hard because he was intent upon teaching them a lesson.

Gloria was impaired in a different way. She was so frightened and insecure that she turned her daughter into a psychological cripple. Eight-year-old Leslie clung to her mother and was virtually unable to function independently.

When I first met her, Gloria told me that because she was so afraid of her ex-husband, Steve, she and Leslie had been forced "to go into hiding" and obtain an unlisted phone number. She declared, "I'd kill him if I saw him; I'd kick his goddamn ass." Because Leslie was terrified that her father might abduct her, Gloria drove her up to the school entrance even though their home was just across the street from the school. Gloria and Leslie devised a "code" whereby if Leslie phoned from the school office to report she forgot her lunch, her mother would rush over. In fact, Steve had never been sighted near the school. School administrators suspected that Gloria was exaggerating the danger and turning her daughter into an emotional wreck. Leslie's academic performance was faltering, and she didn't have a single friend. When a school counselor questioned Gloria about the necessity for the extreme precautions, Gloria threatened to inform the superintendent that the school was failing to protect her child. To me she asserted, "The teachers are starting to turn on Leslie; the school isn't listening to me."

Leslie seemed so identified with her mother that she echoed Gloria's inflection and often her words. She asserted that she would shoot herself rather than live with her father. Comparing her situation to that of a guinea pig who would perish if removed from its mother, Leslie remarked, "It's like you can't live without your mother."

Just one month into my evaluation of this case, I became alarmed. Leslie was tearing skin off her arm, had run out of school to be with her mother, and was complaining constantly of aches and pains. A physician who attempted to examine her informed me that Leslie was "hysterical, screaming, out of control, refusing to cooperate with the exam." A psychiatrist Leslie had met with for several sessions described her as unable to involve herself in treatment because she was in "chronic crisis" and was "overwhelmed" by her situation. Leslie's mother seemed to me explosive, uncompromising, and often irrational. Having taken leave from her job because of a psychiatric condition, Gloria had her own therapist, who described her as "a person who seems to stagger from crisis to crisis."

I did not yet know enough about Leslie's father to recommend an emergency change of custody to him. I composed a memorandum to the judge who had heard some preliminary matters in the case, listing my concerns and recommending that Leslie be immediately removed from her mother's care and placed in a more stable environment where she could receive intensive treatment. The judge didn't make any immediate change. He wanted the allegations against the father to be investigated and all parties to be evaluated further. He thought the mother had been put on notice through my memorandum and might modify her conduct.

Every step of the way Gloria tried to convince me that Steve was a criminal who aimed only to make life miserable for her and cared nothing about his daughter. These assertions turned out to be groundless. Steve was a soft-spoken, rather laid-back man. He felt sorry for Leslie, being sucked into her mother's sickness. Steve continued to do his best to set Leslie at ease during her brief visits with him. He never said an unkind word about her mother, nor did he quiz her about her mother's activities. During my evaluation Steve calmly and patiently responded in a straightforward fashion to the allegations that Gloria leveled against him.

When the judge ordered that Leslie live with her father and that her mother's visits be supervised, Gloria declared she preferred not to see Leslie at all rather than adhere to the court's conditions. Imagine what would have happened if Gloria had remained the primary custodial parent! Leslie would have become further enmeshed in her mother's web of paranoia and fear. Eventually she may have refused any contact with her father. And her own emotional health would likely have deteriorated further.

After a number of months Steve realized that, whatever Gloria's flaws, Leslie missed her mother. Consequently he agreed to Gloria seeing Leslie without supervision. Gloria took this generosity for weakness and continued to work on Leslie to live with her. Charging that her daughter had been unwanted and mistreated by her father, Gloria eventually filed for custody. The court denied her petition because Gloria seemed unchanged and Leslie was thriving under her father's care. In my report to the judge, I wrote: Leslie "comes across as a remarkably different youngster, a person virtually transformed. Today [she] is a . . . slender, good-looking, articulate teenager who looks you in the eye, tells you what [she] thinks, shows evidence of a sense of humor, attempts to maintain perspective—a teenager on [her] way to becoming an adult."

There are situations in which a child needs to live apart from both parents. This may occur when one parent is impaired but has made the child so afraid of the other that he can live with neither. This was the case with thirteen-year-old Melvin, who had been so traumatized that he clung to and protected his mother while remaining deathly afraid of his father. The child had become caretaker of the parent. Melvin's world completely revolved around his mother, Sally. He attended school but was failing nearly every subject, behaved in a silly, immature manner, and did not have a single friend. The boy's father commented, "[Sally] wants him as a protector and friend. She had him sleeping in the same bed until a year ago. . . . He'd kill anyone who got in her way."

Although this may seem to be a wildly exaggerated view, the pathologically close mother-son tie was also noted by more objective observers. Melvin's physician stated, "He went to his mother, who rubbed his back as she did several times during the exam. There was much physical contact between mother and son during the examination. . . . Although I am not an expert in psychology, it would be my impression . . . that this is abnormal." Melvin's psychotherapist was more outspoken: "I'm concerned about how they relate—how they behave in the waiting room—his inappropriate affection and kissing or pushing—very inappropriate; that's just not right between a boy and his mother. . . . It's what I've seen at [a psychiatric hospital] with severe kinds of pathology. . . . The mother has a hard time differentiating her wars and [Melvin's] battles."

Sally had enlisted her son as her ally in a war against his father, whom she called "the alligator." Melvin had completely internalized his mother's theory that there was a conspiracy in which, to gain custody of him, his father had "bought off" neighbors, doctors, and others. During the custody evaluation I eventually became included as a member of the conspiracy, especially because I questioned Sally about her beliefs. "You don't care if this child and I starve to death," she asserted. Sally felt even more certain that I had become an enemy after she spotted me in the corridor of the courthouse, where I was waiting to testify about another case. She waved papers at me and implored me to testify in a hearing dealing with the family's financial affairs, in which she was claiming that her ex-husband was trying to force her and her son into the street. When I explained that it would be a breach of courtroom procedure for me to barge into a hearing, Sally pleaded, "Just go in and speak." Shortly after this she became irate that I doubted some of the charges she had leveled against her ex-husband. "You better believe this child," she told me. "You act like this child is a liar. You are insinuating I'm the cause of all this."

Living with his mother, Melvin was being psychologically destroyed. (Sally had even acknowledged that her son was so confused that, in taking a shower, he did not know what to wash first.) But Melvin could not be placed with his father because he was so terrified that he vowed to run away if he had to be alone with him. Having evaluated the father, I did not find Melvin's fear to be grounded in reality. Still, I thought it would be detrimental to force the child to remain with a parent under these circumstances. Melvin's therapist and I concurred in recommending to the court that he be placed in a therapeutic boarding school. I went a step further by recommending that Melvin's custody be transferred to the Department of Social Services. "This will be necessary to help stabilize the environment for Melvin and will insulate him from any attempt to interrupt his education and treatment. . . . Once Melvin is placed, he probably should not see either parent for several months while he adjusts. Eventually, he would be permitted to see his mother. This examiner recommends that supervised visits on campus with his father be considered." I also strongly recommended that Melvin's mother receive professional help.

Trying to reach an accord with an impaired spouse like Frank, Gloria, or Sally is incredibly frustrating. Unless the impaired spouse is in such a deep hole that he or she feels compelled to change, a problem solver's efforts to do what is in the best interest of the child will be thwarted. Consequently, the child will spend much of life in two radically different environments and may be endangered in one of them.

Courts cannot change personality. However, a judicial ruling can get the attention of an impaired parent who is acting in ways detrimental to a child. If all else fails, a problem solver should have his or her attorney go to the court to address the difficulties. A judicial ruling that the impaired parent finds repugnant may shock him or her into owning up to problems and seeking professional help. Losing contact with one's child can crash through denial and be a powerful incentive for change.

Two Controlling Parents

When both parents have controlling personalities, pursuing custody of their child becomes a high-stakes contest perceived in stark win–loss terms. The issue is more bolstering their self-esteem than it is their child's welfare. Both parents deploy tactics honed during a lifetime of trying to wrest control. These tactics require little forethought, for they are automatic expressions of people determined to have their way. They include

- Attempting to destroy the other parent's credibility by lies, smears, and innuendo
- Refusing to communicate
- Withholding information
- Rebuffing criticism by launching an attack
- Capitalizing upon flaws or weaknesses in the other parent
- Trying to humiliate the other parent
- Blaming the other parent for anything that goes wrong
- Subverting the other parent's authority
- Undermining plans the other parent has made
- Causing the other parent to incur additional legal costs

Controlling parents fight over nearly every conceivable aspect of the child's life—money, location of the child's belongings, bedtime, content of television programs and films the child watches, choice of school, selection of academic programs, participation in extracurricular activities, religious education, contact with relatives, medical decisions, the need for counseling.

Controllers routinely engage in character assassination. They record events in meticulous detail and use the information selectively. One father maintained computerized records documenting the foods his wife served their daughter during a five-month period. His purpose was to show that his wife was so incompetent she couldn't be trusted to fulfill even the most basic parental duties. One might wonder that he didn't have better ways to spend his time. If the child's diet was poor, why didn't he do something about it? The answer was that he really didn't care what his daughter ate. His objective was to get the goods on his wife. Some parents use a camera or tape recorder to amass evidence. In one case, whenever the parents exchanged their son, each showed up with a camera to film what the other did. The bewildered five-year-old was in tears every time they met. Some parents hire a private investigator hoping to turn up incriminating evidence.

Controllers attempt to turn neighbors, friends, and relatives against their spouses, then use them as witnesses in court. Using phone, fax, courier, e-mail, and regular mail, these parents deluge their attorneys, mental health professionals, and custody evaluators with information. Nothing is spared as one spouse attempts to defeat the other. One means is running up legal costs. There are many ways to do this, such as alleging abuse, which requires investigation and causes a delay in legal proceedings.

These cases may drag on for years. At the time of this writing, I have been involved for nearly eight years as two parents battled over their four children, one of whom has now graduated from college. Judges despair as mothers and fathers use the courts to play out their personal vendettas.

Lynn and Guy's fight over custody of nine-year-old Jenny exemplifies how vicious two controllers can become. The stack of boxes of legal correspondence, memoranda, court filings, and other documents in the case was nearly two feet high. The parents locked horns over nearly every aspect of their daughter's existence, from her religious education to her shoe size. Each charged the other with keeping secrets to the extent that Jenny's health was jeopardized.

Lynn lashed out at Guy for secretly taking Jenny to a doctor, then ripping the label off her medicine bottle to conceal the name of the prescribing physician.

Confrontations became physical. According to Lynn, Guy blocked her vehicle from entering a pickup zone at school. Guy approached her with a note but asked to talk before handing it over. Lynn declined to discuss anything and warned that she would scream if he did not leave her alone. Guy challenged her further, whereupon Lynn yelled "Rape." Calling her an "asshole," Guy left. Lynn asserted that Guy endlessly engaged in "litigation, allegations, harassment, and intimidation." Citing his wife's angry, unyielding nature, Guy explained that to resolve anything he had to keep taking her to court.

After nearly two years of bickering and a staggering legal bill, the parents finally agreed to joint custody, with Jenny residing primarily with her mother. These were the two longest years of Jenny's life.

A Controller and an Impaired Parent

An impaired parent may be an easy target for a controller who characteristically capitalizes on others' weaknesses. Having lived with the impaired parent, the controller knows his or her shortcomings well enough to use them to his advantage. Instead of trying to work with the impaired spouse or to get that person help, the controller uses the disability or handicap to legitimize having total authority over the children. The attempt is to minimize the other parent's role in the child's life, as if that individual had little or nothing to contribute. I have interviewed children who are despondent about having so little contact with a parent who, however impaired, is still their mom or dad and deeply beloved.

Ellen was a very controlling wife and mother. She became even more so when she realized her husband's psychological problems and some of the things he had concealed. Years before Fred had dropped out of several graduate degree programs, then settled for far less in his career than he had envisioned. Over the next decade Fred experienced bouts of severe depression, during which he became suicidal. His sexual misconduct got him into one difficulty after another, although he was never arrested. It started when he was a child, when Fred spied on his mother while she undressed. As a teenager he deliberately bumped into women and tried to touch their breasts. During his marriage he used his job to make sexual advances. Ellen began to find evidence that Fred was sexually involved with other women.

Eventually Ellen took the children and left the marital residence. Although nothing specific had ever come to light about Fred having a sexual interest in children, Ellen believed that, considering all that had surfaced, anything was possible. Seeking to protect the children, she hired an attorney. Once the judge listened to her concerns, he granted a temporary order that the children's visits with Fred be supervised. He also ordered that both parents have a psychological evaluation.

Fred stated that his wife was angry at him and out of revenge was "trying to exclude me from parenting." This was not new, he contended, pointing out that for years his wife had displayed contempt toward him in front of their children. Fred complained that his wife continued to make decisions without consulting or notifying him. Ellen insisted that anything he wanted to say should be in writing, then she would reply in writing. Fred asserted, "She wants to destroy me and will use the children; it's unconscionable."

I understood Ellen's apprehension about Fred. So much had been concealed over many years that there was no telling what remained buried. And it was true that, for reasons not yet clear, one of the children did not want to spend time with Fred. Ellen took the children to several psychologists to be evaluated for sexual abuse. All of the mental health professionals concluded that neither child had been sexually abused by their father. Although Ellen expressed relief, she clung to her belief that sexual improprieties had occurred between Fred and the children. Fred was evaluated by a psychiatrist and found to have no pedophilic inclinations. The fact that Ellen would not relent in her insistence on supervised visitation suggested that she was enacting her own agenda to pay her husband back for his years of betrayal. The controller was using her husband's impairment to drive a wedge between him and his kids, one of whom he was very close to while the other seemed to be imitating her mother's rejecting attitude.

Two Impaired Parents

When both parents are severely impaired, a child's best interest is unlikely to be served. The case of Molly, Greg, and their two daughters is one in which it is hard to imagine the children having anything other than a bleak life.

Greg depicted his wife as a mentally ill individual who had "no sympathy for those in pain and sickness" and could be cruel to both human beings and pets. He claimed that she was psychologically scarred by the fact that, when Molly was a teenager, one of her brothers shot their parents to death. Greg also reported that Molly had been raped several times by family members. He contended that his wife had never dealt with these traumas. In court Molly testified that she had seen spirits. Greg asserted that she was unfit to care for their daughters. Moreover, he was alarmed by her threat that, once she gained custody, she would severely limit his time with the girls.

Molly in turn characterized her husband as abusive, incompetent, and untrustworthy, and avowed that Greg was on the verge of losing his occupational license. She said that for seven years Greg had refused to participate in marriage counseling. It was obvious Molly was determined to convince me that her husband was an unfit parent and a pervert. Describing her husband's sexual behavior before their marriage, she stated, "He'd come into my apartment and take my clothes off and masturbate on top of my body." During a six-month period of their marriage, Molly claimed that Greg refused to have sex with her unless she was asleep. She described other erratic and bizarre conduct by Greg: He turned off the heat in the house and, as the temperature plunged to forty degrees, resorted to using a kerosene heater at his bedside. Molly contended that the girls didn't feel safe with Greg. She stated that one daughter would go into a panic if left alone with her father: "I could not run to the store or take a private moment unless [she] was asleep." Not only did her husband neglect the children but, Molly pointed out, he often failed to change his clothes and the house looked like a pigsty.

This is a typical adversarial custody case in which one parent slams the other. But both these spouses had psychological problems and few parenting skills. The children were residing with the mother, who had been the primary caregiver. Initially the judge appointed me to evaluate the mother so the court could "be satisfied that she suffers from no mental disease that is in any way detrimental to the children." He later changed the wording from "mental disease that is in any way detrimental" to "mental disorder that in any way places the children in jeopardy."

This was one of these cases in which every interview, whether with mother, father, or one of the children, gave rise to more questions than answers. Testifying in court, I discussed the mother's psychopathology. However, the basis for the judge to reach a decision rested on the definition of the word *jeopardy*. Finally the judge narrowed the question to whether I thought one day he would read in his morning newspaper that the mother had "boiled the children in oil." My answer was no. This was not an endorsement of Molly's parenting skills or personal stability but a direct reply to a narrowly focused question about imminent danger. It was certainly true that Molly had some unconventional, if not bizarre, beliefs, but I could not conclude that these rendered her dangerous to her children. The judge's decision was to leave them with their mother. I cannot honestly say whether the children might have been better off staying with neither impaired parent.

You can tell a lot about a person just by observing and listening under relatively innocuous circumstances. Playing cards with him, riding as a passenger while she drives her car, watching how he treats his spouse at a work-related function all provide clues about personality. A person is what he is and, over time, he will reveal himself ever more fully. If a man or woman reasons logically, considers and values opinions different from his or her own, and is willing to compromise for the benefit of others, he or she probably will not approach child custody by girding for battle. If the individual values winning above all and seeks to dominate and control others by any means, expect him or her to enter the custody arena in full armor with weapons at the ready.

It is of critical importance to the resolution of child custody whether a parent functions primarily as a problem solver or a controller, or suffers from a debilitating impairment. You have lived with your spouse for years. As you deal with him or her in divorce-related matters, you need to think realistically about how he or she has approached other conflicts in life. Evaluating your spouse in an objective manner will be of inestimable help as you try to work out what is in your child's best interest.

If You Are a Problem Solver Divorcing a Problem Solver

- Focus on your child's needs first and foremost.
- Make an effort to see things from your child's point of view.
- Despite your negativity toward your spouse, treat him or her as a positive force in your child's life.
- By being receptive and flexible, demonstrate that you want to resolve differences in a civil fashion.
- If you reach an impasse, iron out differences through a mediator.

If You Are a Problem Solver Divorcing a Controller

- Do your utmost to ignore personal attacks and stay focused on your child.

- Be firm, but try to avoid anger.
- Confront lies, distortions, and exaggerations with facts, not emotions.
- Don't be afraid to point out that, by waging a battle against you, your spouse is actually harming the child whose best interest he or she claims to be serving.
- Utilize neutral professional resources such as a mediator or guardian ad litem.
- If you find yourself becoming frustrated and emotional, talk with your attorney rather than react and regret what you say or do.

If You Are a Problem Solver Divorcing an Impaired Parent

- If your spouse refuses to acknowledge a severe impairment, you may need to have an expert attest to its existence and severity and its impact upon your child.
- Ask your attorney to request a psychological evaluation or an independent custody evaluation.
- Inform your attorney of any evidence of the impairment so that he or she can subpoena documents (e.g., medical or therapy records) or witnesses (such as therapists or witnesses of particular events).

If You Recognize Yourself as a Controller

- Ask yourself what's more important—making your spouse suffer or caring for your child?
- Don't make life more difficult for your child by putting him in the middle and subjecting him to a test of loyalties.

- Bear in mind that waging a perpetual vendetta against your spouse may rob your child of the only childhood he has.

- Realize that attempting to destroy your spouse psychologically or financially will only hurt your child.

- Consider that your uncompromising attitude will inflict untold misery on everyone, yourself included, perhaps for years.

- Remember that everyone benefits by cooperating; everyone suffers in a war.

- Resolve to be open to suggestions and proposals—consider their merit rather than automatically rejecting them.

- While dealing with your spouse, focus on substantive current matters, not on old grievances.

- Think about how spending your life in litigation will take a huge toll in time, money, and emotional energy.

- Remind yourself that squandering financial resources through a protracted custody battle will leave less for your child's future.

If You Recognize That You Are Impaired

- Disclose what the problem is. Admitting to a problem is a critically important first step in trying to resolve it.

- Relate what measures you have taken in order to resolve the problem.

- If you have done little so far to address the difficulty, state clearly the specific steps you will take.

- Do not regard seeking help from others, notably trained professionals, as a weakness. Rather it is an indicator of insight and a desire to improve.

- Bear in mind that if you are impaired but continue to deny it, your child will suffer.
- If an independent professional or a judge concludes that you have a serious problem, pay close attention to what you are being told. These are people who want to help you and thereby help your child.

III

The Pursuit of
Child Custody

No matter how much strife has filled your marriage, your life has had a certain routine flow. Once the decision is made to separate, everyone has many adjustments to make. Your child has to live somewhere and with someone. It is fantasy to think that his or her life will remain the same except for inhabiting two homes instead of one. In most cases the youngster will need to make one place or the other home base. Having to divide time between two parents makes for a life radically different from anything your child has known before.

As you become involved in the process that will ultimately decide where and under what circumstances your child will live, you are likely to find yourself in foreign territory. When custody issues are contentious and the differences must be litigated, few parents are prepared. Unless you are a domestic relations attorney, the world of motions, pleadings, interrogatories, depositions, and court hearings will be totally unfamiliar to you. In this section of the book, I'll help you navigate the realm of lawyers, mediators, evaluators, and judges. Understanding the legal options for custody is critical because the type of custody you end up with will have far-reaching ramifications for you and your child every day, perhaps for many years.

Before pursuing a particular type of custody, consider three things very carefully. First, examine your motives. Are you seeking to get back at your spouse? Are you trying to amass as many days of custodial responsibility as you can primarily to pay little or no child support? Are you looking at the outcome in terms of a personal win or loss, as a report card evaluating your success as a parent, or even as a validation of your overall self-worth? This is a time for total honesty. In truth, you probably have mixed motives. Where does your child's best interest fit in? Second, think about the time, energy, and money you'll expend in a custody battle. I have seen parents plunge themselves, their own parents, and other relatives into debt while fighting for custody. This money could have been better used drawing interest in a college fund for the child. Finally, reflect on the life you want your child to have. Whatever the pressures of the legal arena, don't lose sight of who your son or daughter really is and what he or she needs.

If the custody case goes to trial, a judge will decide what is in the best interest of the child. Reaching that opinion means ascertaining the child's needs and how well each parent is able to meet those needs. The factors judges consider are similar from one jurisdiction to another and generally include the following (from the Code of Virginia Domestic Relations 20-124.3):

1. The age and physical and mental condition of the child, giving due consideration to the child's changing developmental needs

2. The age and physical and mental condition of each parent

3. The relationship existing between each parent and each child, giving due consideration to the positive involvement with the child's life, the ability to accurately assess and meet the emotional, intellectual, and physical needs of the child

4. The needs of the child, giving due consideration to other important relationships of the child, including but not limited to siblings, peers, and extended family members

5. The role which each parent has played and will play in the future, in the upbringing and care of the child

6. The propensity of each parent to support the child's contact and relationship with the other parent, the relative willingness and demonstrated ability of each parent to maintain a close and continuing relationship with the child, and the ability of each parent to cooperate in matters affecting the child

7. The reasonable preference of the child, if the court deems the child to be of reasonable intelligence, understanding, age, and experience to express such a preference

8. Any history of family abuse as that term is defined in Virginia Code Section 16.1-228

9. Such other factors as the court deems necessary and proper to the determination

Chapter 4

Types of Child Custody

THE TWO IMPORTANT questions regarding child custody arrangements are With whom will the child be living? and Who will be making the decisions? In terms of benefit to the child, the name for the type of custody is less important than the schedule and how well the parents get along. My practice is in Virginia, but the terminology for custody arrangements may vary from state to state. A label given to a form of custody may be determined by considerations such as calculation of child support and not the number of days a child lives with a parent.

There are two types of legal custody: sole and joint. A parent who has **sole custody** makes nearly all the decisions about the child. He or she may be required to consult with the other parent, but sole custody confers final authority in decision making. Parents with **joint custody** share decision making.

Under sole custody, the child lives primarily with one parent, who essentially has complete legal authority in the child's life. The noncustodial parent spends time with the child, a frequent arrangement being every other weekend and alternate holidays. Depending on circumstances there may be a midweek visit for dinner or even an overnight visit during alternate weeks. It is usually the sole custodial parent's obligation to provide information to the other parent and to seek the other parent's views on important matters. Sole custody is necessary under the following circumstances:

- One parent is not physically available to care for the child, for instance, when a parent has no fixed address, is incarcerated, or for other reasons can have only minimal contact with the youngster.
- A parent is so impaired physically or psychologically that he or she cannot care for the child.
- A parent has a history of neglecting or abusing a child. In such cases, if time is to be spent with the child at all, it is likely to be only with a supervisor.
- An individual is a parent in name only—in other words, professes to love the child but is largely unaware of the child's needs because he or she has been uninvolved in the youngster's life.

A sole custody arrangement may be necessary when one parent repeatedly refuses to communicate and cooperate with the other, letting matters hang in limbo so long that the child may have to miss opportunities. For example, if one parent doesn't tell the other of his or her preference for weeks of visitation during summer vacation, the youngster may not be enrolled in camps, sports teams, or community activities. One parent having sole custody makes it possible to resolve such impasses.

A warning about sole custody! It can be a powerful weapon in the hands of the wrong parent, i.e., a controller who would attempt to block the other parent from participating in the child's life.

Sole custody does not grant permission for one parent to ignore the other and decide everything unilaterally. A responsible, conscientious parent with sole custody communicates with the other parent, provides information, seeks advice, and demonstrates an accommodating attitude.

Janice had launched a vicious, although ultimately unsuccessful, two-year campaign to prove Elmer an unfit and abusive father. When the judge awarded him sole custody of his daughter, Elmer could have exploited this authority to get back at his ex-wife. However, he didn't perceive the judge's decision as a personal victory. Seeing Janice leave the courtroom in tears, Elmer remarked, "Nobody really won." Because he put his child's needs first, Elmer wanted to repair the parental relationship. Consequently his first initiative was to invite Janice to join him and his daughter for dinner once a week.

If there is to be a co-parenting agreement, and in many cases there should be, the *schedule* of spending time with the child is more important than the name given to the arrangement. If both parents are to participate actively in the child's life, the process to make this occur must be defined. For co-parenting to work, the parents must have demonstrated in the past and currently that they can communicate and cooperate.

Joint custody is intended to ensure that a child maintains a close relationship with both parents. This arrangement presumes that both parents want continuing involvement in the child's life and will share responsibility for meeting the child's needs and making decisions. Many time divisions are possible under joint custody. A child may spend equal time with both parents, switching at designated intervals. Generally, however, a child experiences less upheaval with one home base, where he or she sleeps, keeps most school supplies and wardrobe, and, at least on school days, has a relatively predictable routine.

In an article titled "Children and Divorce," Kenneth Jost and Marilyn Robinson observe, "Joint residential custody arrangements often prove to be expensive, emotionally wrenching, logistical nightmares for parents and children."* They note a trend toward designating one parent in the joint custody arrangement the "primary caretaker." I have recommended this arrangement on many occasions. The fact that one home is identified as the child's primary residence does not diminish the role of the other parent, who is to have equal say in matters such as health and education.

There are many variations of joint custody. In one instance the mother and father lived a thousand miles apart, and the judge ordered what he termed "modified joint custody." The child resided with the mother during the school year. Adding up most of the summer vacation weeks, designated three-day holiday weekends, and alternating Christmas, Thanksgiving, and spring vacations, the father also spent a great deal of time with the child. By order of the court, each parent had decision-making power during the time he or she spent with the child. The parents were to consult each other on major decisions and to share information about schooling, health, and other activities.

For any form of joint custody to be successful, the parents must agree to frequent contact to share information and discuss decisions. Joint custody is most viable if each parent truly believes and

---

* Kenneth Jost and Marilyn Robinson, "Children and Divorce," *CQ Researcher,* vol. 1 (June 7, 1991), pp. 349–368.

acknowledges that the other has an important role to play in the child's life.

Joint custody is far less likely to work when it is imposed by the legal process on parents who remain angry with each other.* Impasses can occur because of failure to communicate, cooperate, and achieve closure on matters requiring decisions. In one instance, it took a judge to order that a father could have additional visitation time to take his daughter to piano lessons. Seven months later the little girl still had not had her first lesson because the parents failed to agree on dates. The last I knew the father was threatening to return to court to resolve the issue.

Despite the likelihood of continual wrangling, joint custody may be the arrangement of choice when one parent is trying to exclude the other or when one parent feels defeated and is about to drop out of the child's life. It may be the only legal means to ensure that the child can maintain a close relationship with both parents. To make certain that decisions get made, final authority can be vested in one parent while retaining the designation of joint custody.

Although intimidating and domineering with his spouse, Grace, Phil was a devoted and sensitive father. He sought to minimize Grace's contact with their two children and had a history of thwarting her visits and obstructing phone access. Although their father was the more involved and competent parent, Grace had a great deal to offer. I worried that if Phil had sole custody he would feel empowered to limit further Grace's participation in the children's lives. Calling the arrangement joint custody but giving Phil final decision-making power

---

* Bruce A. Copeland, "Judicial Criteria for Applying Joint Physical Custody in Litigation Cases" (unpublished).

was intended to send him an ongoing reminder that the children needed the involvement of both parents in their lives.

Shared custody is a variant of joint custody. In some states it is determined by a specific number of days during which a child resides with a parent. Shared custody requires that parents be flexible in apportioning the time each spends with the child. Very young children need to see both parents frequently. They do not yet mentally carry the image of the absent parent as they will when they are older. Because their time is not structured by school, there is more opportunity for allowing infants and toddlers frequent contact with both parents. Shared custody, especially for preschoolers, is the best arrangement if both parents are problem solvers who are not combative with each other. It will be a nightmare if the parents are controllers.

In one situation, even though both parents were controllers, I took the unusual step of recommending a 50-50 custody arrangement. The two preschool-age youngsters had a strong emotional attachment to both parents. Because they were suffering from the family breakup, I did not want these very young children to sense that they also were losing one parent in a custody arrangement. The children weren't in full-time preschool, and the logistics of dividing the time equally between parents who lived within a short drive of each other weren't terribly burdensome. Once the parents separated, their relationship was far less volatile. Despite their charges and countercharges during the custody evaluation, they commented positively about each other and emphasized the importance of each being involved in their offspring's lives (even though each wanted to be the primary custodial parent). The judge asked how the arrangement that I recommended could work given that both parents were controlling and had difficulty communicating. I replied that each had voiced a strong desire to improve their relationship by going together to consult a professional who would help them communicate better. The judge then implemented my recommendation.

Shared custody for children whose parents live close to each other may make psychological as well as logistical sense. One sixteen-year-old expressed no preference for a primary residence because he had strong relationships with both his mother and his father. Although the parents were extremely different in personalities and attitudes, each contributed a great deal to the boy's life. Despite disliking each other, each parent respected the teenager's desire to maintain a close relationship with the other. Pleased that he did not have to make a choice, the youth divided his time, bicycling between the two homes. His mother and father continued to be meaningful parts of the boy's life without having to compete.

There are situations in which a child spends time with a parent only when a neutral third party is present. This is known as **court-ordered supervised visitation** and occurs mainly if a parent has physically or psychologically endangered a child. I have yet to meet a parent who acceded willingly to supervised visitation.

A five-year-old boy had been throwing tantrums and vomiting before each visit with his father. The father blamed the mother, contending that she had been turning the child against him. He asserted that once his son left the mother, he was no longer distressed. The mother was perplexed and upset because her son was averse to spending time with his father. An evaluation revealed that the father had neglected the physical needs of his young son, grilled the child about his mother, and constantly disparaged her and her friends. The boy told a psychologist he wanted to see his dad but only if someone else was present. The psychologist recommended that he continue visiting his father under supervision while the father received psychological help. Infuriated, the father told his son that he would maim the boy's psychologist so that he would not be able to walk. The court ordered the father to hire at his own expense a mental health professional to supervise the visits.

Sometimes parents agree upon a relative, friend, or other person to supervise visitation. Otherwise the supervisor is an impartial individual, such as a social worker, pediatric nurse, teacher, or representative of a church to which either parent belongs. For a fee some agencies provide qualified professional supervisors. The supervisor is to be independent, neutral, and nonintrusive but present at all times during every visit. He or she is to report observations to a therapist or custody evaluator, or to testify in court. If the parent requiring supervision significantly improves, the court-ordered supervision requirement may be dropped.

Supervised visitation is intended to protect children. However, it can protect parents in two ways. If allegations have been made in the past, supervisors may be in a position to report that, based on their observation, they see no basis for them. The presence of a supervisor may be a deterrent to new allegations. If a new complaint is raised, the supervisor was right there to witness what really happened. If he or she does not substantiate the new charge, light is shed on the malevolent intent of the accusing parent.

The Washington Post reported in 1998 that some divorcing parents are developing unconventional custody arrangements in order to reduce trauma to their children.* For example, parents change

---

* "Custody and Compromise," *Washington Post,* December 14, 1998, p. A1.

places by moving in and out of the marital residence for equal time periods. The child stays in the familiar home and neighborhood, keeps the same friends, and does not have to change schools.

In his novel *The Boy, the Devil and Divorce*, Richard Frede describes a custody battle that culminates in just such an arrangement. With their marriage crumbling, the Whitneys build a spectacular new home. The "golden couple with the golden boy" decide to end their marriage. The attorney for the child advises the court, "The marriage may have failed, but the divorce should be a success." He recommends what he believes to be in the best interest of Justin, who is age ten at the start of the custody struggle: "The intent of the proposed order . . . is to minimize the breakup of Justin's family structure and to allow him to benefit from the mutually reinforcing relationships he has previously enjoyed with both parents. I am advocating that Justin spend equal time with each parent, but in a continuous environment."* The attorney proposes that the house be placed in trust for Justin until he turns eighteen or finishes high school, whichever occurs later. He then asks that the parents "alternate monthly residence with the child" and recommends that "the parent in residence pay the bills accrued during residence," while both parents share general maintenance costs and taxes for the home. It is a solution in which the "the child has custody of the parents."

This was fiction. I do not personally know of a case in which such an arrangement was adopted, probably because the house would have custody of everyone. I do know a fourteen-year-old who urged his parents to keep the house but alternate living there. He was em-

---

* Richard Frede, *The Boy, the Devil and Divorce* (New York: Pocket Books, 1992), p. 367.

phatic about not wanting to start all over again in a new neighborhood and school. His mother explained that she and his dad needed to have their own places and establish separate lives. Clearly, there are potential serious limitations to rotating in and out of the marital residence, especially once a divorced parent is dating regularly or remarries. But even if remarried, parents who are civil and cooperative can live on the same street so they are available to their offspring at virtually any time. If parents are truly committed to the welfare of their child, they will find a workable custody arrangement.

Custody agreements need not be irrevocable. Children have different needs at different points in their development. A type of custody suitable for a toddler may turn out to be impractical once the child enters elementary school. Parents who are observant, sensitive, and flexible will voluntarily alter the custody arrangements to conform to their child's best interest.

Chapter 5

Legal Representation

No matter how amicable the separation seems to be, it is usually necessary for each parent to consult an attorney. Sooner or later differences emerge, and spouses need to know their options in order to protect their interests. I am amazed that people take more care buying cars than they demonstrate selecting professionals to help with critical situations in their personal lives. When they're considering purchasing an automobile, they talk to others, consult publications, research on the Internet, take test drives, and comparison shop. I have known parents who hired an attorney because a telephone listing indicated that the office was near their home, or because they'd gotten a casual referral from someone they barely knew. Granted, it's far easier to obtain information about cars than it is about lawyers. However, far more is likely to be at stake in choosing a lawyer than in buying a car.

Always consult an attorney who specializes in domestic relations law. You wouldn't hire a dermatologist to conduct brain surgery, nor should you choose a tax attorney to handle divorce. You need a specialist qualified to help you with the legal issues of divorce: division of assets and liabilities, child custody, and child support. This person must know the law in your jurisdiction and be experienced in handling divorce and child custody litigation from the first filing until the final settlement. He or she should serve as your mentor through the legal maze, offering explanations in a clear, unhurried manner and helping you through legal proceedings such as taking depositions, preparing documents, and attending court hearings.

Finding a domestic relations attorney may require research. Obtain names from relatives, friends, and neighbors who have experience. Word-of-mouth referrals are helpful, although not always reliable. Call the local bar association for names of practitioners. Ask if a given lawyer has any malpractice claims or other complaints lodged against him or her. As you ask around, seek the following information:

1. Is the attorney readily available by phone, and does he or she return calls promptly?
2. Is the attorney not only knowledgeable but also clear in explaining things?
3. Does the attorney follow through on promises or does he or she have to be pursued and reminded?
4. Does he or she do things promptly?
5. Does he or she take on too many clients so that cases languish for lack of attention? Yours could be one that gets put on the back burner.

After completing your research, schedule appointments to interview several lawyers. Some offer an initial consultation without fee. Others charge. Given what is at stake, paying the fee is likely to be worthwhile. Prepare for your interview. Make note of the questions you want to ask and points you need to make so that you're organized when you meet. Rather than deluging the attorney with details, present the essence of your case. Don't hesitate to ask specific questions about how he or she would approach your case. Ask the following questions about the attorney's practice.

- How long have you been in practice? (You don't want a novice; you're looking for someone with several years of practice who has handled dozens of divorce cases.)
- What are your fees, and do they vary with the task (e.g., drafting documents, interviewing witnesses, appearing in court)?
- How much experience do you have in mediation? In courtroom litigation?
- How available will you be? What are your regular business hours and what is your availability by telephone outside those hours? If you're out of town, does someone stand in for you?

Availability is particularly critical because emergencies don't limit themselves to weekday working hours. One father flew to a midwestern city for his regularly scheduled weekend visitation with his son. Upon arriving, he called his ex-wife to confirm the pickup time. Only then was he informed that the child wouldn't be available for visitation because he was ill. However, the boy's mother was vague about his condition; it appeared that this was another tactic in her history of obstruction. Told he could not even speak to the child on the phone, the frustrated father phoned his attorney. Even though it was a Saturday, both his and his ex-wife's attorneys were available, and he was able to spend the weekend with his son, who, it turned out, had the tail end of a virus.

Consider the approach to custody you believe will be most beneficial to your child. You know your spouse far better than any lawyer. There is a major difference between a lawyer who primarily offers mediation services and a skilled courtroom litigator. If you are fairly certain that you and your spouse will arrive amicably at an agreement, you may not need the services of a litigator. The problem is that you can't always divine the future. Negotiations sometimes break down, and things can turn ugly. If you're dealing with a controller or impaired parent and the relationship between you and your spouse is growing increasingly adversarial—and especially if specific allegations have been leveled about your fitness as a parent—retaining an experienced trial attorney is essential. Plenty of attorneys know the law, but some are more effective than others in the courtroom. If your spouse has retained a skilled trial attorney but you have chosen a mild-mannered negotiator or an attorney with little trial experience, you are likely to be outmaneuvered.

In the *Family Law Newsletter* Michael Minton has described for his attorney readers the plight of the domestic relations lawyer as he or she takes on a new client: "You are viewed at the outset as a necessary evil, an obstructionist, an impediment, but a necessary helpmate. . . . You were sought out, needed, and hired to intrude into a very special, very private relationship and to negotiate a contract that, by its purpose, is the antithesis of hearts and flowers and all the hopes and plans of 'and happily forever after.' "*

Communication between you and your lawyer must be rapid and clear; you're paying by the hour. One law firm I know provides

* Michael H. Minton, "To Understand and Be Understood—Techniques," *Family Law Newsletter*, vol. 2 (Summer 1999), p. 9.

its clients during the first meeting with a six-page "letter of instruction" covering eleven topics relevant to divorce proceedings.* The client reviews the document, after which client and attorney sign it. Aside from setting forth specific instructions, the letter clearly states that the lawyer realizes how important the client's situation is, and therefore that it is essential that the two form an open, honest partnership to find effective solutions.

Your attorney will guide you through a process filled with unknowns and pitfalls. He or she advises you legally and in some instances personally. An attorney told me of an unwelcome surprise on the day he met his client in his office before walking to the courthouse. She appeared intoxicated, although she claimed she had only taken a bunch of diet pills. Under her mink coat the client was wearing a sleek, bright red dress; as the attorney recalled, it was cut to the navel. It did not take long for the lawyer to conclude that he needed to ask to reschedule the hearing. He found a ride home for his client and later warned her to be sure that she was sober and dressed conservatively for the next court hearing. The best lawyers will advise you not only on the fine points of the law but on appropriate attire and conduct. How you present yourself in court can have an effect on the outcome of the case.

During the relationship with the client, an attorney may unofficially assume roles of confidant, psychological counselor, and social worker. In working with your attorney, however, do not presume that he or she is any of these. You have hired an attorney for the explicit purpose of being your legal expert. Beware of unhealthy

---

* The domestic relations law firm of Gannon & Cottrell, P.C., Alexandria, Virginia.

dependency, which can develop between attorney and client just as in other relationships.

Marge counted on her lawyer for far more than legal assistance, and her growing emotional dependency complicated the attorney-client relationship. Not especially confident to begin with, Marge felt ground down by the custody litigation and suffered panic attacks, headaches, insomnia, and depression. Her sympathetic attorney gave Marge her home phone number. Marge made numerous calls, ostensibly relating to legal matters but actually more to seek emotional support. Occasionally Marge put her young children on the phone to relate their father's latest alleged atrocity. Although the attorney did not charge a fee for every minute of the substantial time spent reassuring and calming her often hysterical client, the fee for all her services eventually exceeded $100,000.

You're paying your attorney for legal expertise, not emotional support. An attorney is *not* a therapist. If you need mental health counseling—and I believe this can be enormously helpful for many people—hire someone in that field to help you.

Be sure you understand what your attorney is saying. Don't hesitate to ask for clarification. If you disagree, let the attorney know immediately. Bear in mind, the attorney is your employee. As in any relationship, being straightforward is preferable to festering in silence. Don't worry about offending the attorney; in all likelihood he or she would prefer that you disclose problems. Failure to do this can impede resolution of your case.

Remain accessible. Your attorney should be aware of your schedule and know how to contact you. Don't expect him or her to do everything. Undertaking as much as you can will save legal expenses. Assemble documents in a timely and orderly fashion. Don't expect your attorney to address every problem you have with your spouse or ex-spouse. When parents resolve conflicts on their own, the savings in time, money, and energy are considerable. More important, knowingly or unknowingly, you'll be laying the groundwork for cooperating with each other in your child's best interest.

In some cases the court appoints a guardian ad litem (GAL), an attorney who represents the best interest of the child or informs the court of the child's preference. Such appointments are made at the judge's discretion and occur more often in some jurisdictions than in others. Some judges appoint a GAL in every custody case. I have encountered GALs in complicated cases with very young children who cannot speak for themselves and in cases where the battle over custody is so ferocious that a judge decided the child needed to have his or her own legal representation. The guardian ad litem may interview the parents, observe or interview the children, make home visits, and consult with other professionals, including the custody evaluator.

Chapter 6

Mediation and Negotiation

Some courts require divorcing couples to participate in activities to educate them about divorce. Many courts, including those in Virginia, require parents to attend seminars that address the impact of separation and divorce on children, parenting responsibilities, and options for conflict resolution. A number of jurisdictions require parents in the process of divorcing to enter a mediation process. Mediators may be specially trained attorneys or mental health professionals who work directly with the parents or with them and their attorneys. Mediation seems sensible, especially with its potential for significant savings in time, energy, and money. Mediation of custody and other divorce-related matters can also strengthen the foundation for trust and cooperation between parents.

In his book *Mediating Child Custody Disputes,* clinical psychologist Donald T. Saposnek points out, "Mediation is not therapy or counseling. It is a highly structured process for negotiating a temporary or initial agreement from which later decisions can be more rationally made."* At the time of his writing, nearly twenty years ago,

---

* Donald T. Saposnek, *Mediating Child Custody Disputes* (San Francisco: Jossey-Bass, 1985), p. 48.

California required that custody cases go to mediation before judges would allow them to be heard in court.

Frequently, my contact is with divorcing couples who refuse to participate in mediation, or for whom mediation has been unsuccessful. Months or years after the heat of the custody battle has subsided, some parents are amenable to resolving other difficulties through mediation. Conflict over custody arrangements may be only a prologue to further discord during years of child rearing. Parents squabble endlessly over their children's education, religious upbringing, participation in activities, and a variety of other matters. Anticipating this, judges may order (in some joint custody cases) parents to consult a mediator if they fail to reach agreement.

Mediation of matters arising during divorce is quite different from mediation of other types of disputes. If there is conflict over a business contract, the issues are usually clearly definable and amenable to a finite resolution. However, issues that emerge during marital breakups are complex, and new difficulties keep arising, especially as changes occur in family members' circumstances and in the needs of the child. Resolution of conflict through mediation is most likely when both parents function together as problem solvers; controllers and impaired parents usually have to be dragged down this path.

Collaborative Family Law

Collaborative family law offers another approach to avoiding courtroom fights. Instead of a third party mediating, each parent retains a lawyer with the sole objective of resolving divorce and custody issues. The attorneys agree in advance to withdraw if the case moves into litigation. The collaborative enterprise commences before either client is served with divorce papers. Describing this process in *The Matrimonial Strategist*, Stu Webb, a Minneapolis family lawyer, writes: "By definition, the collaborative lawyer is a settlement specialist. . . . If settlement is the client's goal, a collaborative lawyer can serve as a coach to guide the client through the process. . . . The lawyers and their clients have to learn to leave their anger and resentment at the door."★

Some people erroneously believe that the act of hiring an attorney guarantees a protracted battle. This is not necessarily true. An attorney can insulate you from some of the emotional intensity of dealing directly with your spouse and restrain you from making unwise decisions. Most domestic relations attorneys are ethical. They are not seeking to drag their clients into gladiatorial combat. In fact, the attorney you retain is likely to do his or her utmost to resolve conflicts without going to trial. In its standards of conduct, the American Academy of Matrimonial Lawyers has taken the position that attorneys should negotiate, mediate, or arbitrate marital disputes. An article in the association's newsletter points out that one of their standards (2.15) specifically "recognizes the existence of increasing evidence of the destructive effect of protracted adversarial proceedings on the child and encourages the cooperative settlement of child custody disputes."★★

Even if their clients are already engaged in warfare, conscien-

---

★ Stu Webb, "Collaborative Law: An Alternative for Attorneys Suffering 'Family Law Burnout,' " *Matrimonial Strategist*, vol. 13 (July 2000), pp. 7–8.
★★ M. K. Kisthardt and B. E. Handschu, "Effective Techniques for Counseling the Client Seeking Custody," *Matrimonial Strategist*, vol. 17, no. 2 (December 1999), p. 3.

tious attorneys endeavor to help them subordinate emotion to reason, tone down the hostilities, and move toward a settlement. If both clients are working to resolve problems rather than defeat each other, their attorneys will help them reach an agreement. The resolution of divorce issues becomes memorialized in a consent order, which the parents sign without having to participate in courtroom litigation. A consent order is a legal document simply stating what the parties agree to. It is signed by the attorney for each parent, then by a judge.

Chapter 7

When Mediation Fails:
Preparing for Custody Battles

W<small>HEN TWO PARENTS</small> dislike each other intensely and agree over very little, mediation generally fails. A civilized process is needed to determine what is in the best interest of their offspring. The next step is to the courthouse to resolve the custody battle. Some problem solvers, who would vastly prefer to negotiate rather than spend enormous amounts of time and money fighting, find themselves dragged into fierce custody battles by a controlling spouse. If both parents are controllers, they relish tactics to vanquish the other parent, including making unfounded allegations. If one or both parents are impaired, the custody battle can result in painful accusations of mental instability or unfitness to parent. Unfortunately, the hallmark of most custody battles is one parent's attempt not to present his or her qualifications as a fit parent so much as to disparage the other parent.

The mother of a young child leveled nearly two dozen allegations against her husband. She claimed that the father improperly fed the boy, unmercifully criticized his son, purchased a gun and threatened to kill both the child and her, refused to help his son with schoolwork, and neither bought his son clothes nor kept his clothes clean. Faced with evidence that these charges were untrue, she did not relent. When the subpoenaed sales records of the gun shop showed that no gun had been bought by the father, the mother asserted that either the records were incomplete or the father had presented false identification to make the purchase. All the mother's allegations were eventually proven untrue. But everyone lost! The mother lost custody. The father lost hours and tens of thousands of dollars disproving the allegations. And, because the son was privy to some of the allegations, his relationship with his father suffered.

Mothers have told me that their husbands have threatened to leave them penniless and take away their children. Fathers have reported that their wives vowed to clean them out of money and possessions, then warned them they would be lucky even to see their children. In making threats and attempting to carry them out, parents lose sight of what is important, and the children become pawns. I have watched couples fight over everything imaginable, including what their child's real name is. In several cases in which I was involved, each parent called the child by a different name.

Evaluating allegations and threats takes place during the process called discovery. And what parents discover is often horrifying.

"Discovery" in Custody Battles

The process of discovery allows each side to have access to information bearing on child custody issues and distribution of marital assets once the couple is divorced. A vindictive spouse may cast a huge net to accumulate evidence that will bolster his or her contentions and destroy the other parent's chances of obtaining custody. Since each parent knows the other intimately, it is practically a given that any flaw, weakness, mistake, or other vulnerability will be exposed, magnified, and capitalized upon.

Through the legal discovery process, each spouse is compelled to answer questions, many highly personal. Documents, including heretofore confidential papers such as the notes of a psychotherapist, are subpoenaed. Private investigators tail a spouse searching for incriminating evidence such as adultery, deviant sexual behavior, unsafe driving habits, alcoholism, drug use, or gambling. One husband had a private investigator follow his wife to her rendezvous with another man. The investigator was able to dash into the room where the couple was having sex and take a flash photograph before beating a hasty retreat. In one instance a wife paid several thousand dollars to have experts scrutinize a computer hard disk to determine whether her husband had downloaded child pornography. Witnesses are corralled to corroborate allegations. One father had had a falling out with his own mother, a fact that was seized upon by his wife. Promising frequent contact with the two grandchildren if she got custody, the mother pressed her mother-in-law to disclose to me information damaging to her husband's custody case. The mother-in-law spoke at length about her disappointment in her son, how awful his new fiancée was, and how he had changed so drastically that she felt she didn't know him anymore.

In preparing its case, each side is able to obtain written legal discovery by asking a set of interrogatory questions. These deal with any personal matter that might be relevant. Another part of the discovery process is taking a deposition, during which opposing counsel questions a parent, whose own lawyer also is present. (The other parent has a right to be present, which I do recommend.) The parent is under oath to respond truthfully, and a court reporter takes down every word. Nearly anything a person has ever done that is illegal or immoral, or that shows bad judgment, can return to haunt him or her. Your driving record, medical records, and prescription history may be scrutinized. The circumstances surrounding any criminal record are likely to be probed in detail. Your financial records are closely examined not only to obtain a detailed accounting of assets and liabilities but also for evidence of extravagance, misuse of funds, or hiding of assets. Your employment history and job evaluations provide evidence of your stability, competence, and responsibility at work as well as verification of earnings and indications of interpersonal problems. In one case a professional person had had so many run-ins with her office staff, colleagues, and administrators that she was required to have a psychiatric evaluation before returning to work. Her ex-spouse brought this up to suggest her unfitness to parent.

Here are critical areas that are fair game during the legal discovery process.

Exposing Psychological Problems

When people consult psychiatrists, psychologists, and social workers, they usually do so with the understanding that what they reveal will remain confidential. During child custody litigation, however, records of mental health professionals are discoverable (meaning they can be opened).

Long before she was married, Margaret voluntarily entered intensive psychotherapy to address personal problems. To her consternation, during the discovery process a mountain of her therapist's notes, covering years while she was single as well as married, were subpoenaed. Margaret witnessed her therapist being grilled by her husband's lawyer in a deposition that her husband also attended. The most intimate and private events of her life as well as her dreams and fantasies became discoverable. Margaret faced the prospect of having to repeat this psychological scrutiny by being questioned and having her therapist testify during the custody hearing.

Sometimes a parent takes the positive step of seeking help as he or she attempts to cope with a deteriorating marriage. During custody litigation, that person's spouse pounces upon his or her being in treatment as evidence of psychological instability or even proof of being unfit to assume custody of their child. (I nevertheless recommend seeking a therapist when necessary for two reasons. First, it will help you. Second, it demonstrates your willingness to recognize and address problems.)

Agnes's situation shows what misery a controller can inflict, driving his spouse to a breakdown, then attempting to manipulate others, including a judge, into thinking he should have custody. Agnes told me that her husband, Bret, had tried to "control and manage" everyone in the family. Their three children were expected to behave like little soldiers. When Agnes intervened to protect the children from Bret's abuse, he ignored her, called her names, or physically assaulted her. Agnes endured what Bret meted out because she loved her husband and thought she could convince him to seek help. Eventually she managed to talk Bret into attending marriage counseling.

Bret seized upon the meetings as an opportunity to enlist the therapist's support and sympathy. Unsparingly, he cited his wife's deficiencies. To Agnes's consternation, Bret's conduct was never the focus. Concluding that the counseling was futile, she told Bret she would not return. Later Bret accused her of sabotaging the chances of reconciling their differences, despite the fact that he had not accepted any responsibility for problems or changed one iota.

Agnes continued in her effort to serve as "the glue of the family." She described life with Bret as "walking on eggshells" and participating in "constant negotiation." Her confidence faltered as she began to think that perhaps, as her husband claimed, she was "this horrible person," especially because she was thinking more and more about ending the marriage.

When her children reached school age, Agnes took a part-time job, gained self-confidence, and became more assertive with Bret. He responded violently. Agnes suffered a black eye, bruises, insomnia, and anxiety and depression so intense that she entered psychotherapy and was placed on medication. Immediately Bret wrote the therapist a letter in which he presented himself as deeply concerned by his wife's mood swings and her "dysfunctional anger." Bret advised the psychiatrist that Agnes was becoming a danger to herself and others, even their children. He urged the doctor to take a "proactive treatment approach" and volunteered to assist in any way he could.

Nearly a year after she entered therapy, Agnes took the children and left the marital residence. She was supported in her decision by family and friends, all of whom had been amazed that she had not left sooner. They understood more about her reticence to leave after Agnes disclosed that Bret had left her penniless by closing all their joint accounts. Until the court intervened, Agnes and the children managed only through financial assistance from her parents.

In what exploded into an ugly custody battle, Bret decided to make his wife's mental health a central issue. He declared that Agnes had reached "the breaking point" and that he could document at least two dozen instances in which she had lost control. Bret advised me that he had filed for custody of the children because "my wife is unfit in her current state." He attributed his children's poor relationship with him to a malicious campaign by Agnes. Bret's lawyer subpoenaed Agnes's mental health and prescription records. On the one hand, Bret espoused benevolence toward his wife, telling me, "I hoped against hope she'd get better" so that the children's "loving relationship" with him could be restored. Meanwhile, he was portraying Agnes as chronically mentally ill with virtually no prospect of recovery. Bret asserted that whatever his wife had accused him of was a projection of her own thoughts and wildly oscillating emotions. He commented, "She's trapped with a horrible illness [and] she hasn't dealt with her problems." Bret demanded that his children be "protected and sheltered from her abuse."

Agnes admitted that, after repeated provocation, she had lost her temper and slapped her husband on several occasions. And she acknowledged experiencing intense "bouts of depression." However, she told me that cause and effect were being inverted in her husband's claim to custody. Agnes's point was that anyone under similar circumstances would have done well not to have a complete nervous breakdown. "I feel very strongly I've been manipulated. . . . I've had periods of depression, but who wouldn't given what I've gone through with him? I've done what's decent and right. . . . How many beatings do you take? . . . I went for help. That was responsible."

The children told me that their father was demanding, unreasonable, self-centered, and difficult to please. One of the boys refused to talk to his father or visit him. Bret attributed this entirely to his wife's influence, then did what was in keeping with his personality: He insisted that his son must be sick and in need of help. The youngster avowed that his negative attitude had nothing to do with his mother, who actually had urged him to have contact with his dad.

I found Agnes not only credible but also a fit parent who was loved and respected by her children. She had a community of friends who described her as a devoted mother conscientiously trying to hold the family together while providing a superb role model for her children. I recommended to the court that the scrutiny of Agnes's mental health cease immediately. Once I submitted my report, and other evidence was before the court, Bret failed in his campaign to gain custody. During the litigation the judge learned of other unsavory aspects of Bret's character and conduct. Shortly after Agnes was given sole custody of the children, Bret left the area, fleeing legal, professional, and financial responsibilities. Above all, he abandoned his children.

Attacking Reading and Viewing Habits

Adults keep some interests and preoccupations to themselves. But a spouse seeking custody may make a case that the other parent is so absorbed by a particular interest, such as viewing pornography or spending time on the Internet, that it will harm the child, either because the youngster is neglected or because he or she is exposed directly to a damaging influence.

One mother became so immersed in the Internet and e-mailing, including flirting with other men, that she paid little attention to her children. While she was riveted to the computer screen, she sat her children in front of the television, which she relied upon as a baby-sitter. This behavior became an issue in the custody case.

Another mother insisted that her husband wasn't fit to have visitation without supervision because of his avid appetite for pornography. After asking him to remove all pornographic magazines from the house, she came upon more of them, including, to her alarm, one with photos of prepubescent girls, stuffed under a couch. She also reported that on several occasions she found her husband masturbating while he looked at pornographic pictures. Recalling that one of these incidents occurred in mid-afternoon, she stated, "My son could have come in at any time." The husband acknowledged that he had magazines with photographs of adult sexual activity. He also admitted that he had masturbated while watching the Playboy Channel. However, he vehemently denied any sexual interest in minors. He stated that the photos of children his wife had found came from a textbook on sexual development that a roommate had purchased fifteen years earlier. "I had the book. Was I obsessed with children? No. I was throwing it out. The book had fallen apart. I'm sorry I didn't throw it all out." Asked why he had saved this particular book, this father replied, "I have lots of books after fifteen years."

The wife sought to prevent her husband from having overnight visitation with the children. She stated, "I was afraid that if he could not stop himself from bringing pornography into the home and from watching the Playboy Channel, that he may not be able to stop himself from whatever might be the next step. Possibly molesting our children or even someone else's children." Because there were young children in this situation, the judge in the case ordered supervised visitation.

Three years later, when I became involved as an evaluator, it was clear that the father had gotten the message. Remarried, he had no pornography in his new household, and he had submitted to a psychological evaluation. No evidence was ever offered that the father had any deviant interest in children. The judge lifted the supervised condition but ordered that the father receive counseling. In granting unsupervised visitation, the judge cautioned the father: "Whenever this court is concerned about the welfare of children, we have not only the power but the duty to address that until we're satisfied that it's fixed. I want you to be clear that no judge in this court will hesitate to do that again."

In another case a wife contended that her former husband should have supervised visitation because he was "addicted" to pornography. Once, upon returning home from a meeting, she saw that her spouse had been masturbating and drinking and then had fallen asleep watching a pornographic film. She was horrified to think that one of the children might have come downstairs to find the father with his pants down and the film on the screen. After the parents had long been separated, the custody case came to court. During my testimony I maintained that the father's earlier behavior did not constitute an addiction although it certainly was evidence of poor judgment. By the time of the hearing, this man had stopped drinking, no longer kept pornography in his house, and was determined never to repeat the objectionable behavior. Moreover, he agreed to consult a therapist and follow his recommendations. The court granted him liberal visitation.

In these two cases each wife had a reasonable concern. However, long past the point where it had been addressed and corrected by the offending spouse, each wife continued to use it as a club to limit the father's access to the children. It took a judge's deliberations to restore the possibility of a normal father-child relationship.

In contested cases the finger-pointing can become extremely petty. One parent reacts to the other allowing their child to watch an R-rated film as though a terrible atrocity has been committed. The child gets grilled every time he is with one parent about what programs or movies the other parent let him see. I'm not an advocate of allowing children to watch a bunch of gratuitous sex and violence. In fact, I discourage it. Even the most conscientious parent may err in judgment and take a child to a movie that gives him nightmares, and you should know that this lapse may come back to haunt you. I find, however, that the attempt to use such an incident to build a case is more damaging than anything a child sees in the movies or on the TV screen.

Focusing on the Family's Living Environment

How you live is a relevant consideration in a custody case. What counts is not how fancy your house is but rather its condition and how safe the home and neighborhood are. There is reality, and then there is whatever exaggeration an unscrupulous parent will make. If a child accidentally falls and is injured in the home, a parent can latch onto this event as "evidence" that the other parent is either negligent or simply unable or unwilling to ensure a safe environment. In one case when the parents separated, the father took "custody" of the family dog. The mother bought a new dog, which bit her daughter. Because his wife did not immediately get rid of the animal, the husband contended that she was negligent. In fact, the dog had been tormented by the child until it bit her in self-defense. The pet didn't have an inherently malicious temperament but, evidently, the child did.

Do you smoke? This habit is bad not only for your and your child's health but for your custody claim. In 1999 the *Brown University Child Behavior and Development Newsletter* cited cases in New York, Louisiana, and Maryland in which smoking was a consideration in child custody decisions.★ The publication noted that the decisions came in the aftermath of research finding that "children exposed to tobacco smoke in large quantities are more than twice as likely to develop lung cancer in the course of their lives." In the Maryland case, an asthmatic child was placed with a foster family because both her parents refused to stop smoking in her presence.

Needless to say, if you drink or have used illegal drugs, these habits will also be scrutinized during custody battles. Where you relocate, temporarily or permanently, after leaving the marital residence will also be examined. After his parents' marriage broke up, a youngster and his mom moved into what seemed to be a group home. The child told a therapist that his mother was seeing a number of men. The psychologist recorded in his notes: "[The child] saw some

---

★ "Smoking Parents and Child Custody Case," *Brown University Child Behavior and Development Newsletter,* December 1999, p. 6.

people coming in and out partially clothed and some drinking. . . . The boy talked about partying and drinking. He was very insecure and angry."

The mother claimed that the home was the best she could afford at the time. Two years later, at the time of the custody suit, she had a far better living situation. In his bid for custody, the father cited the earlier conditions as evidence of his ex-wife's poor character even though he had never objected to his son spending time with her there. Ultimately, the "group home" atmosphere wasn't particularly important in resolving custody. The main issue was that, despite the mother having improved her circumstances, the father was able to provide a far more stable environment, so he became the primary custodial parent.

For financial reasons a parent may rent a room or an entire level of the house to a boarder. The other parent may seize upon this as representing a potential danger even though he knows nothing about the boarder. One mother was apprehensive because a man was renting a room in her husband's home, and he was sometimes on the premises when her eight-year-old daughter visited. I discussed the situation with the father, talked with the child, and interviewed the boarder. I found that actually the gentleman was helpful in many ways. He assisted in maintaining the house, freeing the father to spend more time with the child. Rarely was the boarder around because he spent long hours at his temporary work assignment and left town most weekends to visit his own wife and children. The child liked him but seldom had contact with him. His room had a separate entrance from the outside, and he rarely was in the main part of the house except to join the child and her father for an occasional meal. I saw nothing wrong with this arrangement.

I have been surprised by the number of custody cases in which the presence of firearms in the home has become a subject of intense controversy. In many instances the firearms belong to a parent or grandparent who is a collector or hunter but has demonstrated that he or she is fastidious about safety precautions. The fact that a handgun or rifle is on the premises does not by itself raise a safety issue. Still, assuming the firearms have been obtained legally, critical questions need to be answered: Where are they kept? Are the weapons loaded? Where is the ammunition stored? Who knows of their presence? For what purpose are they used? How emotionally stable are the individuals who have access to them, and how sound is their judgment?

Revealing Sexual Deviancy

Unless a child is at risk, there is no reason for a person's sexual practices to become an issue in a custody case. Of course, sexual involvement with a minor is a criminal act (a felony in many states), and steps must be taken to protect a child. Exposure to a parent's sexual activity clearly is an appropriate concern in a custody case. Beyond this, however, a person's sexual proclivities, even if not regarded as mainstream, need not be a consideration.

Sexual Orientation

If a marriage breaks up because of a parent's homosexuality, how relevant is it to custody? If that person was a good parent before, does the revelation of his or her sexual orientation change that fact? To the spouse who feels betrayed and humiliated, it may.

In one case in which I was involved, the husband initially was furious over being left by his wife not for another man but for another woman. He asserted that his wife was unfit to be a custodial parent because she would raise their daughter in "an immoral and illicit atmosphere." This father also contended that, because of her lesbian relationship, his wife was "unable to devote her full attention to the needs of our [child]." Neither legally nor in good conscience could the child's father set forth a compelling case that his wife was promiscuous or that she would subject the child to harmful influences. His spouse had a monogamous relationship and had no intention of having her new partner move into her home. Their daughter regarded the mother's partner as a much-loved aunt. The facts of the situation virtually compelled the father to acknowledge that his wife had been the primary caretaker of the child since birth and an excellent mother. Eventually he agreed to joint custody and to the child residing principally at her mother's home.

Being homosexual does not mean that a person lacks good parenting skills. (Nor for that matter does being heterosexual render a person a good parent.) Far more important are other personal characteristics, such as empathy, integrity, dependability, and being able to spend time with and care for the child. In a disputed custody case, one parent may contend that the other, who is homosexual, cannot be a good role model, the implication being that the homosexual parent will promote or somehow impose his or her sexual orientation as well as what the other parent considers an offensive lifestyle on their offspring.

An unscrupulous parent may allege that his or her spouse has hidden homosexual interests. One mother did just that when she found out that her husband had taken their son to the beach and shared quarters with a longtime male friend who was not married. She claimed her husband neglected his family, preferring to spend hours on Sundays playing tennis with this same individual; her strong insinuation was that the two were sexually involved.

In speaking with her husband, I determined her claims were untrue. The gentleman in question was a friend of some twenty years whom the mother knew. He was a bachelor who dated a number of women but had never settled down into married life. The quarters shared at the beach consisted of a two-bedroom condominium where father and son slept in one bedroom while the friend slept in the other. There was some truth to the accusation that the father preferred the company of his friend over that of his family on Sundays, but this had nothing to do with a sexual interest. Rather, his wife had made their home life so disagreeable that he sought escape from the tension that arose whenever they were together, which they were on Sundays more than any other day of the week. His spouse's innuendos were part of a campaign to win sole custody. After the expenditure of a huge sum of money and untold emotional grief, her motives were uncovered, and she failed.

Assessing Involvement or Lack of Participation in the Child's Activities

Parents who are involved in a custody dispute often keep score of who goes to what activity or who does what in child care. A parent who has been marginally involved may make an overnight bid to become mother or father of the year as he or she dashes from one activity to the other or becomes newly immersed in mundane chores like dressing, feeding, bathing, or changing diapers for a young child. The motivation for this increased participation in the child's life may stem from a number of factors. It may have the aim of outperforming the other parent. It may be an attempt to curry favor with a son or daughter. Or this new immersion may occur because, after the marital separation, a parent feels alienated from his or her offspring. Regretting missed opportunities, he or she now wants to invest more time to cultivate a good relationship.

Eventually, assertions and allegations often collapse under the weight of facts. A parent's track record as a dedicated caregiver over the last few months may fade under questioning going back to the time the child was an infant.

I recall a professional man who worked twelve-hour days and often on weekends. His wife lived as though she were a single parent, assuming responsibility for nearly all aspects of child care. She was the parent who made sure the children were properly dressed and equipped as they participated in their many activities. She oversaw their homework, conferred with teachers, attended school programs, and became a Scout den mother. If her husband had been asked, he could not have named the children's teachers, identified their pediatrician, or recalled the date of their next sports event. He studied their report cards and praised or chided them about their grades, attended an occasional athletic competition, and went to church with his family, the last mainly for the sake of appearance. Suddenly, during custody hearings he became a superdad who wanted to be part of everything his children did. It turned out that the father's involvement was a cynical and unconscionable ploy to defeat his wife. He had vowed to leave her destitute and take from her what she valued most, the children. The mother obtained sole custody.

The discovery process can take weeks, even months. Discovery proceedings are arduous. You need to be completely candid with your attorney as he or she is preparing discovery documents. Hold nothing back! Your case may suffer if he or she first learns something negative about you from a source other than yourself. Ambushes in the courtroom can be particularly difficult for you and your attorney to handle as they must be responded to on the spot.

When your deposition is taken, you are likely to feel vulnerable because the process is alien and threatening. Despite preparation by your attorney, you will not know in advance specifically what you will be asked. I offer the following tips.

1. Speak up; don't mumble, or you won't project confidence.
2. If you don't know the answer to a question, say so. Don't guess.
3. Answer *only* the question you are asked. Don't volunteer superfluous information.
4. Do your utmost not to take personally the tactics or seeming provocations of the attorney questioning you.
5. Maintain an even and respectful tone in your responses. Do your best not to appear threatened, angry, or defensive.

Chapter 8

Costs of Child Custody Warfare

CHILD CUSTODY BATTLES take their toll—financially, emotionally, sometimes even physically. The purpose of this section is *not* to plunge you into despair or saddle you with guilt. It's to help you stand outside your own anger and grief and anticipate potential adverse consequences of custody warfare. If you're aware of these consequences, you'll be powerfully motivated to move in a positive direction.

In part IV, I will offer specific suggestions on what you can do to minimize your losses.

Financial Costs

The financial toll of a contested custody case can approach or exceed six figures. Without a doubt the fees paid to attorneys, people like myself, and others could be invested to benefit the offspring of divorcing parents. Many times I have commented to parents that the funds being poured into their custody battle could be better spent directly on their children. I would gladly have talked myself out of many jobs as a custody evaluator.

I have heard complaints about the steep legal expenses in custody disputes. Lawyers do not sell a product of unlimited supply. Like other professionals, they have only so many hours per day in which to apply their expertise. They will charge an agreed-upon hourly rate. Working closely with domestic relations attorneys, I have come to appreciate the enormous amount of time spent by these ethical practitioners as they master a huge amount of detailed information. Nothing less than a child's future is at stake.

Although you know your own situation, your case is brand-new to your attorney. At the outset your attorney will spend considerable time interviewing you and reviewing the materials you provide. Preparing motions, petitions, and pleadings to file with the court takes time. As the litigation progresses your attorney is likely to interview witnesses and review more documents. He or she will be involved in preparing and responding to the interrogatories (referred to by more than one client of mine as "derogatories"). Your attorney may spend considerable time traveling to and from court, then waiting to be heard by a judge. (Some courts are experimenting with handling certain matters by telephone to reduce the hours that litigants and counsel lose in waiting.) Depositions, during which the attorney questions witnesses, may consume many hours. A court reporter, who will prepare a verbatim transcript of the deposition, also must be paid. Doing legal research and consulting experts involve additional time and fees.

All of these activities occur before a custody trial takes place. The trial itself is likely to be tremendously expensive. The attorney will spend hours, possibly days, preparing. Not only must he or she review the details of the case but your lawyer must also draft questions for direct examination and cross-examination of witnesses. I have seen lawyers wheel cartons of documents into the courtroom. To have all this information immediately at his or her fingertips while arguing the case, the lawyer or an assistant must spend hours organizing and indexing it all. Your attorney also spends time preparing you and witnesses for trial. The custody hearing itself is likely to last a full day or, if the case is especially complex, many days. I participated in one case that dragged on for nearly two weeks. Each day after court your attorney is likely to be back in his or her office preparing for the next day's proceedings.

If you're a controller, you aren't likely to doubt the correctness of your position. If your lawyer displeases you, you may fire him or her. Some litigants go through several lawyers. Some fail to get along with any attorney and choose to represent themselves. If a judge rules against them, they might regroup so that they can mount an even more ferocious offensive. The financial costs mount just as ferociously.

There may be many costs in addition to legal fees. A custody evaluation by a clinical psychologist can run thousands of dollars. Professionals such as therapists or accountants, who will serve as expert witnesses, charge for preparation and travel time as well as for testifying at trial. A judge may appoint a lawyer for the children, called a guardian ad litem, who will charge an hourly fee. Additional costs may be incurred for long-distance telephone calls, reproduction of documents, special process servers, overnight delivery services, and couriers. Transcripts of legal proceedings, if needed, can be expensive. And you may lose earnings as you take time off from work.

The total amount a parent ends up paying for an all-out custody battle is likely to exceed initial estimates. No attorney entering a case can know how complicated and time-consuming it may become. New conflicts keep surfacing, especially if both parents are controlling people who seek to turn every issue into a battleground. Costs skyrocket when parents refuse to talk with each other and drag their attorneys into the fray on even the smallest matters. Even if one problem-solving parent prefers to negotiate and compromise, he or she may have little choice but to expend funds on litigation to counter the other parent's maneuvering.

Rebecca had become fed up with Ralph's moodiness, controlling behavior, and angry outbursts. She left home with her two young daughters after her husband had struck one of them for touching his computer. After the separation Ralph lost his job and changed addresses often. Because of his erratic behavior, the court ordered him to obtain a psychological evaluation. Rebecca wanted her husband to get professional help so he would settle down and she could trust him with their girls. Instead, Ralph hired lawyer after lawyer, filed one motion after another, and blamed her for his personal, financial, and occupational setbacks. Ralph berated her whenever he came to pick up the children, wrote nasty letters, and left belligerent messages on her answering machine. With her husband hiring and firing attorneys, she was constantly on the defensive and having to pay her attorney to respond and to go to court on her behalf. Because Ralph had a great deal of money, he didn't care how much he spent. Convinced that Rebecca was the source of his problems, he vowed to drain her of every cent she had.

The threat by one parent to spend another into destitution is not necessarily empty. Jeff left Sarah for another woman but still decided to go after custody of their four-year-old daughter, Kerry. Jeff was financially well off and had a steady income. Sarah had maintained a low-paying part-time job while Kerry was in nursery school. Most of the time she was home caring for her daughter. Becoming pregnant with Kerry had taken a heavy toll both in years of emotional anguish and in thousands of dollars spent consulting fertility doctors. Jeff had obtained custody of two children from his earlier marriage, and Sarah had done her utmost to be a loving stepmother to them. Now she was terrified that, with his high-priced lawyers, Jeff would succeed in taking Kerry away from her.

Several weeks before the trial, Sarah's resources and those of her mother were just about depleted. She still had to pay for a psychological evaluation and more depositions. Sarah had warned her attorney that her husband was uncompromising and that the case would never get settled out of court. Sadly, this turned out to be true. Although her husband had agreed to joint custody, he was prepared to go to any length, fighting over the precise number of hours per week that he and his new wife would spend with Kerry. In a near panic, Sarah told me she feared that after the trial she might have to declare bankruptcy. As I write this, eight months after the trial, the judge still has not handed down a ruling.

I have known parents who reluctantly have declared bankruptcy because they could not discharge debts they had incurred both before and during a custody case. The financial aftermath lingered for years, imposing hardship on them, their children, and often their relatives.

Think of everything you want to do for your child. Consider the cost of college, or the ability to help your son or daughter with that first apartment or fledgling business. Is it in the best interest of your child to bleed your financial resources into a custody battle?

Costs in Time

Perhaps no parent contesting custody can imagine how much time he or she will expend on the endeavor. You may spend dozens of hours in consultation with a lawyer, accountant, therapist, and custody evaluator. Hours will be gobbled up hunting for and assembling financial data and other information. Your attorney might request a detailed written narrative of your marriage. The custody evaluator may ask each parent to fill out lengthy questionnaires. Interrogatories require precise information about bank accounts, investments, credit card balances, life insurance, pension plans, outstanding bills, and other financial matters. Contacting people who can provide additional information may take hours. Driving to and from therapy or counseling sessions and waiting for your child can consume several hours each week.

If your domestic situation necessitated calling in the police, child protective services, or other investigative agencies, you may spend hours arranging for interviews, responding to questions, and leaving follow-up messages for people who aren't readily available by telephone.

Going to and from court and waiting in court devours hours. A half-hour hearing may require an hour or more in travel time and then an entire morning of waiting until a judge is ready to hear your issue. For more lengthy proceedings, I have known parents to spend the better part of a day waiting around the courthouse, only to have the case rescheduled. The court's docket is overcrowded. An emergency situation usurps time from the custody hearing. A judge is sick, and all the other judges are busy. A judge declines to hear the case, reserving it for another judge who is already familiar with some of the issues.

In busy city courts the whole process may break down. I recall one case in which the judge started the custody hearing two hours late, then encouraged the parties to reach a settlement. The case went forward, but not without several interruptions for the judge to attend to briefer and apparently more pressing matters. At one point she left the courtroom for three quarters of an hour. Upon returning she warned the litigants that once the two days set aside for the case were exhausted, it might be months before the court's docket would have room for her to hear more testimony and conclude the proceedings. Some witnesses had flown in from out of town, and it was unlikely that they could all be convened again. Contemplating the inconvenience, the financial cost, and the emotional toll of a delay, the parties negotiated a settlement. One of the lawyers quipped that if one were to add the hourly fees charged during the time wasted as the attorneys and expert witnesses sat twiddling their thumbs during that one day, the sum would exceed what some families work months to earn.

Not to be overlooked as a major expense is the time you and your attorney will spend preparing for the final custody trial both on your own and on the attorney's clock. Having to prepare for a custody trial may seem odd, given that you know the situation intimately. But the litigating attorney counts on you to assist in organizing information as he or she prepares the case. And if you are going to take the witness stand (which is likely), you must be ready to deal with a totally foreign arena—the courtroom. Fumbling for information or appearing confused would detract from your testimony. Your attorney may rehearse the questions he or she will ask you, then subject you to a mock cross-examination. He or she will coach you in how to conduct yourself throughout the trial—everything from how to dress to how to keep your composure while being grilled by the opposing attorney.

Most parents find that attending to legal matters requires taking time from their jobs. During business hours you may have to make and receive calls that pertain to your case. Some employees avoid or postpone taking on a new job assignment because they know they won't have the time to devote to it. I have met men and women who have passed up opportunities to advance their careers because of the demands of a custody battle.

Emotional Costs

In a custody battle the parent who is a controller is focused on winning. His or her self-esteem rises and falls depending on who prevails in any given situation. The controller professes to be a reasonable person who desires to reach an accord, but he or she rarely looks at life from anyone else's point of view. Despite assertions to the contrary, he or she is not inclined toward negotiating.

Being tough, persistent, and uncompromising may have helped the controller succeed professionally, but he or she has paid a price for these characteristics in personal life. I have yet to meet a happy controller. Moreover, during divorce proceedings that controller will inflict additional misery, grinding down his or her spouse emotionally, capitalizing on the slightest sign of weakness. The child is victimized because of the tribulations endured by battle-fatigued parents. Remaining constantly on the defensive leaves both parents jittery and exhausted, detracting from the attention and care devoted to the youngster. Sometimes the controller's behavior is so egregious that a judge must intervene.

One judge became alarmed over reports of a father's repeated temper tantrums when he picked up his son for visits. The father's outbursts at his wife were so fierce that the judge put a temporary halt to the visitation. The father blamed his spouse and told me that by lying to everyone, including the court, she was destroying his relationship with his son. He vowed to expose his wife's duplicity so that the court would restore and eventually expand the time he could spend with his child. His wife, who was not a controller, continued to suffer. She was constantly being dragged into court by her husband, who didn't care how much time or money it cost. Her fear of him intensified because every time the court ruled in her favor he became more enraged. One day she called me because her husband had said he was considering moving into her apartment complex so that he could see his son every day. Fortunately, this turned out to be an empty threat.

I have heard all sorts of accusations by irate controllers. The judge is biased against mothers. The judge is biased against fathers. The opposing lawyer must be in cahoots with the judge. Declaring that an entire county's court system was biased and corrupt, one father threatened to have the U.S. Attorney General's Office investigate. When the court put a halt to his visitation and ordered him into therapy, this father spent his time with the therapist complaining about his ex-wife and the courts. He took no responsibility for what had happened.

Catching a parent off guard, ambushing him or her with something totally unexpected, is part of the controller's strategy. The problem solver remains apprehensive, not knowing when it will again become necessary to drop everything to deal with a new crisis that the other parent has precipitated. There are always further allegations requiring a response. Did you take your child to an R-rated film? How long did you leave her in the car alone when you dashed into the cleaner's? Did you send him to school in a pair of tennis shoes that had a hole? Every aspect of what you do is under a microscope, and your spouse is just waiting for you to misstep.

Conscientious parents have told me how upsetting it is when a spouse refuses to take responsibility for his or her misconduct and instead blames the child for any conflict that arises. During the custody evaluation, Gary warily talked about his father's constant grumpiness, his pushing him to try out for athletic teams, and his getting so angry that he would yell until he was red in the face. When I attempted to speak to the father about his son's distress, he became evasive and defensive. I learned later from Gary that his dad told him that any complaints were to be voiced to him, not anyone else.

When the family was together, Gary's mother had insulated him to some extent from his dad's irascibility. But after the marital separation there was no buffer. In his constant anxiety about disappointing his dad, Gary's self-confidence began to erode. During the custody fight, this man was claiming to be the better parent. Bolstering his own image was obviously more important than considering that he could be a source of his son's difficulties.

During a custody battle two controlling parents are like trains barreling toward a head-on collision. Each continues on the track ready to derail the other, but it's the child who is strapped down on the railroad ties. Many times I have seen parents shamelessly vie for their child's attention by scheduling simultaneous activities the youngster wants to enjoy. The child is forced to choose; quite unnecessarily, and to the child's detriment, he or she is faced with a test of loyalty. Whatever the child opts for, he or she risks disappointing the other parent. Were the mom and dad asked, they would be shocked at the suggestion that they had done anything that might cause distress to their offspring!

Sometimes the parent will use the child as a mouthpiece. I intended to talk with six-year-old Arnold after I had interviewed both of his parents. However, I received an urgent call from his mother insisting I give Arnold an immediate opportunity to tell me about how his father had mistreated his three-year-old brother during the last visit. Not knowing how serious this situation might be, or whether I might even have to call protective services, I decided to interview Arnold while his recollection was still fresh. I urged the mother not to discuss in advance anything her son might convey.

Arnold reported that their dad had slapped his little brother for instigating fights. Upon further inquiry I learned that he'd slapped the boy several times. When I asked Arnold to demonstrate the slap, he lightly tapped his wrist with his other hand. Arnold told me that both he and his brother enjoyed visiting their father. He volunteered that after the slapping his brother was fine. When I interviewed the father, he denied slapping either child. Months before my involvement in the case, he had filed a petition with social services against the mother for beating Arnold, an allegation that was never substantiated.

When I told the mother that Arnold didn't describe anything

to warrant my notifying the authorities, she seemed disappointed rather than relieved. She asserted that Arnold must have clammed up because he wasn't sufficiently comfortable to tell me all that had happened. Imagine the stress on Arnold, being used as a personal emissary to "deliver the goods" on his father.

Perhaps the most distressing series of events I have watched unfold during custody litigation is the aftermath of one parent falsely accusing the other of sexually abusing their child, then programming the child to believe it happened. In my experience these allegations are nearly all made by mothers who know full well they are deploying what one father termed "the atom bomb" of weapons. If they have not been able to cut their spouse out of their child's life before, this accusation may well do the job. The pressure for the accused to stop living at home is enormous, especially when a government agency becomes involved. While the investigation is in process, the father's contact with the child is drastically limited or halted. He has the formidable task of proving a negative—that the sordid criminal acts did not occur.

In *Divorced Dads,* psychologist Sanford L. Brewer cited and lamented the damage inflicted when allegations of abuse are made. He observed, "The court usually takes the position that even if the allegations are flimsy, it is better to be safe than sorry." In other words, the person making the allegations appears to have the benefit of the doubt because the court is intent upon protecting the child. Dr. Brewer noted that in cases of baseless allegations, "The person charged is powerless to rehabilitate his reputation."★

★ Sanford L. Brewer, *Divorced Dads* (New York: Jeremy P. Tarcher/Putnam, 1998), p. 205.

A mother may attempt to destroy the father-child relation-ship because she wants total control over the child. Allegations may emanate from a child saying something a mother misconstrues. No matter what the evidence amounts to, she becomes aware that she has a powerful new weapon to brandish. The children named as victims of sexual abuse during custody battles are likely to be preschoolers. These youngsters are suggestible, not verbally articu-late, and they usually cling to their mothers. While dependent upon and therefore under the influence of the accusing parent, they are interviewed repeatedly by social workers, mental health profession-als, and in some instances law enforcement agents.

As I was beginning one custody evaluation, Barbara empha-sized how eager her three-year-old was to talk to me. No sooner did she step out of my office than Alan dashed in from the waiting room and announced, "Daddy doesn't live with us because he touched my private parts." Alan told me that his father had slapped his rear end and his penis, scolded him for being bad, and directed him never to tell his mother. It was highly unusual to encounter a child so eager to tell a total stranger what most boys and girls would have to have dragged out of them.

I asked Jake, Alan's father, to be in my waiting room when Bar-bara delivered Alan for his next interview. After Barbara left my of-fice, Alan rushed to his dad and embraced him. Then father and son talked and laughed. After the meeting Alan asked his dad to walk him to his mother's car, where, as it turned out, Barbara was waiting to drive her son to another mental health professional to get support for her case.

Jake told me that when they had lived together Barbara in-creasingly took charge, to the point that she excluded him from bathing, changing, or feeding Alan. She made it difficult for him even to hold or play with their son. Tearfully, Jake recalled Barbara's phone call informing him that she and Alan were at her mother's and warning him that he would never see his son again unless he admitted to sexually abusing him and sought professional help. Knowing he had done nothing wrong, Jake still had to undergo a Child Protective Services investigation, then wait weeks for the report. Finally, the welcome news arrived. In a letter the agency informed him of its determination that the allegations were unfounded. Jake also passed a voluntary lie detector test. But these vindications did not resolve his difficulty gaining access to his son. Barbara rejected the finding, saying the agency study was superficial. She contended that Jake was such a skilled liar that she wasn't surprised he had deceived the polygraph.

Jake feared the outcome of Barbara's unrelenting campaign to convince their son that he was some sort of monster. Meanwhile, Barbara had persuaded both her own and Alan's therapists that the abuse had occurred, and she had placed Alan in psychotherapy to be treated for post-traumatic stress disorder.

Jake's lawyer advised him that, despite the finding of Child Protective Services, he should visit his son only in his wife's presence in order to protect himself from further allegations. From Jake's perspective, his wife had complete power to determine whether, when, and under what circumstances the visits would occur. Because of the tension between Barbara and Jake and the conflicts that occasionally erupted during visits, I recommended that Barbara remain at home and a trained social worker be present at all father-son visits. This professional supervisor observed Jake and his son being appropriately affectionate, having fun together, and generally enjoying a very positive relationship. He reported overhearing Alan confide to his father on one visit, "I believe you didn't touch my private parts."

After months of investigation, which included my having many interviews with each parent and Alan, and interviewing grandparents, neighbors, and preschool staff, I prepared a report and made recommendations. It turned out that Barbara had numerous problems of her own, including unresolved issues about possible abuse when she was a child. Not only was Barbara blinded by her own psychological problems but she also lacked common sense in some of the most fundamental aspects of child rearing. Alan was so tied to his mother, he'd scream whenever Barbara left the room. When he had trouble sleeping, Barbara would encourage the insomnia by playing a favorite videotape, even if it was three in the morning. She was totally indulgent in her desire never to displease her son. Yet she attributed to Jake and his alleged abuse her severe difficulties managing her son.

I recommended to the court that Jake assume sole custody of Alan, that Barbara have supervised visitation, and that the entire family participate in therapy. Barbara's response was to leave the country with Alan. After a year, she told Jake she'd return if he agreed to joint custody. He had to promise there would be no legal recriminations. Desperate to see his son, Jake capitulated. The last news I had was that a therapist was working with the child and both parents.

Although Barbara's abduction of Alan was an extreme measure, the other events in this situation were not unusual for custody cases in which sexual abuse is alleged. The child becomes the originating point for the investigation. His or her contact with the alleged abuser is diminished or temporarily terminated. Talking to investigators who are total strangers, the boy or girl is pressed to provide graphic and embarrassing details about what allegedly transpired. The youngster may be whisked off for humiliating and scary physical examinations. No matter who makes the false allegation of child abuse, the child suffers as well as the innocent adult.

While they attempt to substantiate their false allegations, I consider it a form of child abuse itself for parents to subject children to embarrassing and confusing interviews by mental health and law enforcement professionals or to humiliating, frightening examinations by doctors. Can you imagine how your child would feel being questioned about whether a parent fondled his or her genitals? Or being given "anatomically correct" dolls to enact what happened to him or to her? How about having his anus examined for rectal tearing or her vagina examined for penile penetration?

A father concluded that his wife's boyfriend had molested their four-year-old daughter. To induce her to get in the car so he could take her to a doctor, he told her they were going for ice cream cones. Instead, she found herself in a medical clinic, subjected to what turned out to be a traumatic gynecological examination. Both the physician who examined the child and Child Protective Services declared the abuse allegation to have no basis. Months later, the little girl continued to have nightmares about the experience and was petrified at the prospect of visiting a doctor's office. Two years after the examination for child abuse, the child's psychotherapist stated, "She has never recovered from the fact that she had this exam with no preparation and no mommy." Another dismaying outcome was that the mother's friend, who was totally innocent, had to await the results of the investigation in order to clear himself with the police and the Department of Social Services.

One parent can allege anything against the other, using the

child as pawn. Most children are confused and distraught. In some instances a child knows the allegations are false and takes what may be a high risk in standing up to the parent making them. Daphne's father was determined to prove that his wife was a drug user, a liar, and a prostitute; in other words, totally unfit to be a custodial parent. It drove him into a frenzy when his outspoken daughter told him that she wanted to continue living with her mother.

Although under pressure from her dad about what she should disclose to me, this spunky nine-year-old was quick to relate that her dad "tells me to repeat that he, my sister, and me are family, not my mom." Daphne reported that during a ten-day visit her dad spanked her for mentioning that she missed her mother. She complained that she often had to sneak calls to her mom because her dad did not want her phoning. Tearfully, Daphne said, "My grades were up. Now they're going down. I think about it [i.e., her parents fighting] during my schoolwork. I can't think right. Dad says, 'What can I do to help?' I say, 'Stop putting me through this.' He says, 'I can't.' He doesn't want to!" Daphne's courage served her well. Her mother got sole custody of her, and her father was permitted to see her only under supervision.

A 2000 article in the *Matrimonial Strategist* notes that parents knowingly make false allegations but rationalize doing so as "a legitimate ploy that they must use to obtain or resist custody."* It is an attorney's nightmare to have a case fall apart in court when the client, whom the lawyer has believed, is unmasked as perpetrating a fraud. The *Matrimonial Strategist* points out that some states "specifi-

---

* "Dealing with a Client's Accusations of Abuse or Neglect," *Matrimonial Strategist*, vol. 13, no. 4 (May 2000), p. 5.

cally penalize the making of false or unsubstantiated accusations of child abuse or neglect." I can only hope that more states will follow suit. Moreover, false accusations have become so pervasive that they can obscure the investigation of the most horrible situation: real child abuse.

The costs of custody wars are high. And they can be ongoing. Beyond the immediate financial and emotional drain, these battles can exact tolls on all parties for years to come, particularly if they poison the atmosphere between two parents who must share decisions about their child. Remember these costs—and particularly the smaller shoulders that must bear them—as you proceed.

Chapter 9

Custody Evaluations

A CUSTODY EVALUATION is conducted by a mental health professional appointed directly by the court or agreed to by both parents. It can help clear up a murky situation in which parents are pitted against each other and the case shows no signs of resolution. The evaluator observes the parents and their children under a variety of conditions and is not limited by the rules of evidence in a formal courtroom hearing, as the judge is. The evaluator works not on behalf of either parent but to recommend what is in the best interest of the child. The cost for his or her services is shared equally or apportioned based on each spouse's ability to pay.

A custody evaluator is likely to have had more personal contact with the parents than the judge has. And he or she will have evaluated the child, whom the judge is not likely to meet at all. (Rarely do judges put children on the stand. Once in a while a judge may interview a child privately in his or her chambers.) The final product of the custody evaluation is a set of findings and recommendations. The evaluator may make the report in writing or deliver it orally to attorneys, possibly on the record to a court reporter.

At the beginning the custody evaluator is faced with what

may seem like an enormous jigsaw puzzle and no idea what the pieces will eventually form, or even how many pieces are needed. He or she is stepping into the lives of complete strangers. Before the process is over, he or she will know some of their most intimate secrets.

Initially, the custody evaluator is apt to hear such contrasting and confusing accounts from the parents that it sounds as though each is describing a different family. The evaluator steadily probes beyond the contradictory "he said, she said" assertions. The objective is to develop an in-depth understanding of the personalities of the parents and their children. What is their psychological makeup? How do the parents and child perceive themselves and get along? What are the primary emotional attachments? Who has been the primary caretaker? How well-equipped is each parent to meet the psychological, educational, social, and other needs of the child? How likely is each parent to cooperate with the other in sharing information and consulting before making decisions? To what extent does one parent promote or interfere with the child's relationship with the other parent?

The evaluator assesses each parent and child by conducting interviews, administering psychological tests, making direct observations, and possibly visiting the home. Stepparents are assessed, and stepbrothers and stepsisters are interviewed. The evaluator studies school records, medical records, mental health reports, and legal documents, including pleadings, responses to interrogatories, and transcripts of hearings or depositions. Collateral sources provide additional information. Particularly helpful are individuals who can be expected to be impartial, such as teachers, school counselors, pediatricians, therapists, and social workers. The evaluator interviews others who know the child and the parents well enough to provide information based on direct observation rather than on what has been filtered to them by self-interested parties. Despite their possible bias, relatives may provide useful information because they can recall details of specific events. Their observations may be especially valuable if they have been extensively involved in the care of the child or have spent a lot of time at the marital residence.

I have seen how ready people are to be helpful when the issue is the welfare of children. Although some collateral sources have their own agendas, most try to be as objective as they can. They recognize the difficulty inherent in my job. A child care provider once said to me what scores of people have expressed over the years, a sympathetic "I wouldn't want to have your job. Good luck and God bless you."

Educators, pediatricians, relatives, neighbors, baby-sitters, clergy, and others are likely to be interviewed for their observations. Because their input cannot be kept confidential, they are in a difficult position. Most desire to be helpful, but they don't want to imperil their relationships with family members. Knowing that his observations wouldn't remain confidential, one man nevertheless spoke openly about his next-door neighbor having parties with women spending the night. He confided this information because he was worried about the impact of the father's activities on the children. After the litigation had concluded, with the mother retaining primary custody, this neighbor was confronted with a father "flipping out" over what he had said.

Neighbors, especially those whose children are playmates of the child of the divorcing couple, may be very helpful. They see and hear things while driving car pools and having the child visit for meals or overnight stays. They know the community in which the child is being raised and have seen him or her participating in activities. One neighbor was extremely helpful to me as she vividly described the surroundings in which a mother I was evaluating lived with her three children. She characterized it as a "family-oriented" neighborhood with lots of young children and stay-at-home mothers. Boys and girls played around a cul-de-sac and were treated to special activities, such as the Memorial Day parade, the July Fourth celebration, ice cream socials, and block parties. The community had a pool, tennis courts, areas set aside for skating, and trails for bicycling. The children navigated from house to house with plenty of adult supervision seven days a week. This sort of information is important to a custody evaluator considering where it is best for a child to spend time.

The evaluator may interview friends who have known the feuding parents over the years—buddies from childhood, college roommates, housemates from the days of being single, longtime tennis or golf partners, and work associates who have become friends. Interviewing parents' job supervisors and reviewing written performance evaluations aid in assessing personality. It is not uncommon for employees to be rated on qualities such as dependability, personal accountability, and effectiveness in dealing with co-workers, clients, or customers.

Very occasionally a parent will ask me to speak with his or her spouse from a previous marriage. This is likely to happen when a parent is on the defensive and wants to demonstrate that recent poor conduct is stress related and not reflective of his or her basic personality. Wally's current spouse attempted to depict him as a secretive, controlling person. To refute what she was saying, Wally referred me to his first wife, who was no longer bitter about losing custody of their son when the child was eight. She had a great deal that was positive to say: "He was very good about letting me know what was going on. He's very responsible and has confidence in himself. I didn't feel he was slighting me or being spiteful. I never thought I'd be sticking up for him."

I have also had a parent refer me to the biological parent of his stepchildren. Chad had two objectives in asking me to talk to his current wife's ex-husband. He wanted to demonstrate that, contrary to what his first wife was claiming, he was generous and easy to get along with. Chad also wanted me to know that even his stepchildren's dad would vouch for him as a good parent. Sure enough, the dad confirmed that he always got along with Chad, whom he said was a "nice guy who will do anything for you." He praised Chad as a stepfather and volunteered that he thought Chad had done a wonderful job with his own son, who was the focus of a prolonged custody fight.

The entire process of a custody evaluation is threatening. Baring your soul is hard even when confidentiality is guaranteed and far more difficult when there is no confidentiality and the stakes are so high. Throughout a custody evaluation the prospect looms of dirty laundry being aired. At every meeting with the custody evaluator, you feel as though you are being judged. There is the perpetual quandary of how honest to be. You want to make a good impression. The risk of making what could be seen as self-incriminating disclosures seems enormous because you can't foresee what the evaluator will make of them.

The best advice I can give you is don't try to create a particular impression. Everyone has shortcomings and has made mistakes. Owning up to them is a plus. If you have serious problems, the evaluator's job is to consider whether you're addressing them. One father revealed his depression and occasional heavy drinking. He had been attending meetings of Alcoholics Anonymous and taking medication that would make him ill if he succumbed to temptation and drank. Because he acknowledged his problems and was doing something about them, his ex-wife's efforts to cite them as reasons to impose supervised visitation failed. One mother was taking medication after having been hospitalized several days for depression. She told me about this mainly because she was certain that her husband would use it as a reason to deny her custody of their three children. I conferred with her inpatient doctor and her outpatient therapist. This woman had returned to work, was continuing psychotherapy, and seemed stable. There was no reason she could not share custody with her husband.

A child's response to a custody evaluator depends on several factors. Usually the child fears appearing disloyal to one parent or the other; being forced to choose between a mother and father carries a heavy and unfair burden. Caught in the midst of parents' fighting, the youngster may fear being enlisted as an informant. Then the child fears that something he or she discloses may get back to that parent, hurt Mom's or Dad's feelings, and make a parent angry. With so much at stake, a child may attempt to divert discussion to any subject other than the parents. One girl's parents had been divorced for nearly two years, but they were again battling over custody. Quite aware of the issues and mindful of the adults' sensitivities, she shifted to a more neutral topic. Asked about specific events of the week involving her mom and dad, she began by reporting, "Nothing's been totally bad or totally good." Then she prattled on about what her pets were doing.

Other children are relieved to unburden themselves. They have bottled up their emotions and are eager to confide in someone outside the family. One boy told me, "There are some things I can't say to people. I picture you like one of my brothers and say what I want to say." Talking to a neutral person whose job is to listen often helps children assimilate what has happened. Nine-year-old Carl's world fell apart when he learned that his parents would be living apart. Still trying to absorb recent events, Carl told me, "I never knew this would happen. I thought they'd be married their whole life." This unhappy boy yearned for his parents to reconcile, but he knew that they were headed for a divorce. "Only a miracle could stop these two," he lamented.

Although I don't ask children whether they prefer one parent over the other, sometimes they volunteer this information. If so, their statements require careful evaluation. Young children are particularly susceptible to manipulation by parents. Even teenagers may have experienced years of parental attempts to turn them into allies. My job is to listen and see the world from the child's point of view. The youngster has the opportunity to express how he or she feels, including voicing whatever complaints he or she wants. During a custody evaluation he or she can confide in a professional who is neutral and whose sole job is looking out for the child's best interest.

Some boys and girls clam up during custody evaluations. Their belief that they must be totally fair to each parent limits what they will say. More than one child I've dealt with has figured out the precise number of hours he was spending with each parent, then told me how the custody should be altered so that time would be shared equally. The compunction to be "fair" sometimes precludes a child's revealing important information or disclosing preferences.

It is difficult to discover what a child really thinks if he or she has been influenced by one parent about what to disclose. The same is true if the youngster is so dependent on a parent that he or she fears saying anything negative will jeopardize the relationship. Ten-year-old Gordon lived mainly at his mother's. She was extremely outspoken in denouncing her ex-spouse, and Gordon took it all in. He declared to me, "I wish when my parents got divorced my dad lived in Australia so I wouldn't have to deal with him." Asked why he felt this way, Gordon did not come up with specifics but vehemently exclaimed, "I'd like to make him eat barf and poop. I'd shove it down his throat." Eventually I found out Gordon's chief complaint was really that he wanted *more* of his father, who didn't spend enough time with him and pay him enough attention. He was delighted when his father decided to take him on a trip, just the two of them, for a week.

If your family is going through a custody evaluation, it's important that you avoid the temptation to discuss with your child what he or she will say or has said. How you instruct your child depends on his or her age and maturity. Essentially you need to convey that he or she will be talking to someone who helps families with problems and, in particular, boys and girls whose parents are no longer together. Ask your child to answer any questions the best way possible and tell the evaluator how he or she feels. It will be to your disadvantage if the custody evaluator believes you have tried to influence what your child says. If your child feels constrained in any way, the custody evaluator may not obtain an accurate picture, and your child won't receive the help he or she needs.

Evaluators differ in how far-reaching their recommendations are. Some present only their psychological findings. Others make general recommendations. And still others make detailed recommendations about every aspect of custody except child support or other financial matters. The custody evaluator does not supplant the judge. He or she provides information that can assist a judge. In my experience, after I issue my report and recommendations, most cases do not go to trial. The parents and their attorneys adopt those recommendations (perhaps with minor modifications) or use them as a starting point for negotiating a settlement. If a settlement is reached so that the parties don't have to battle it out in the courtroom, the savings in money, time, and emotional energy are enormous.

There are cases in which the parents fail to reach an agreement. One or both question my findings and object to my recommendations. The case then goes to court, and I testify as an expert witness. There may be challenges to my procedure, to my conclusions, or to my recommendations. I respond to the attorneys' examination and cross-examination. The judge may ask me questions, as may the guardian ad litem (the lawyer for the children). The judge then considers my testimony along with other evidence that is offered during the trial and decides what weight to give it.

Chapter 10

The Courtroom

BECAUSE OF MOVIE courtroom dramas and television programs featuring judges actually holding court, the courtroom is somewhat less of an unknown to the average American citizen than it once was. Nonetheless, for most individuals court is where other people go to resolve their problems. It's not a place they expect to be on trial themselves. For strangers on television to have their private lives exposed is one thing. Finding their own private lives exposed is another matter.

As parties to a legal action, mothers and fathers generally find the adversarial legal process intimidating. There is no privacy, and they find themselves under fire by very personal attacks. As daunting as the atmosphere may seem, a courtroom proceeding guarantees a civilized process to resolve differences for people who otherwise might have behaved in an uncivilized manner.

There is no such thing as a jury trial for divorce or custody proceedings. All such matters are heard by a judge. Consider the position of a judge presiding over a custody trial. He or she has to render a decision that will profoundly and indefinitely affect the lives of people he or she doesn't know. A former chief judge in a court where I have frequently testified used to begin by urging the parents to avoid the trial. Before the lawyers made their opening arguments, he would ask the litigants to go into the hallway and try once more to reach a settlement. He warned that there was a good chance that, if he had to make the decision, both parents would be unhappy. Nonetheless, they and their child would have to live with it. He then temporarily recessed the hearing.

A judge who urges parents to settle a case is looking out for the child's best interest. He or she knows that feuding parents may become even more polarized after a courtroom battle. After ordering a parent to return her children to the marital residence from out of town, a judge admonished both the mother and father about what they would be in for if they continued at each other's throats: "Frankly, if you think this was bad, if you think this was unpleasant, you have not seen anything. Wait until this gets to a full custody hearing."

When the custody trial begins, each lawyer makes an opening statement, not launching into detail but rather stating his or her perspective, outlining the major points. After the opening statements, one or both attorneys may ask for a rule on witnesses. The judge will likely order that anyone who will testify is to wait outside the courtroom and not discuss the case with anyone. The attorneys may then have brief motions on particular aspects of the case or procedural matters. Then the heart of the trial begins as each attorney presents his or her case and calls witnesses.

It is essential that when you appear in court your physical appearance and demeanor communicate respect for the judge. You do this by dressing neatly and modestly (not necessarily fashionably) and by exercising emotional self-control. While sitting through the proceedings, you may become angry at what you see and hear, especially if you believe your spouse, a witness, or the opposing attorney has not been truthful. *At no time* is a display of anger appropriate or helpful to your case. You will do best if you have attended carefully to others' testimony, so you are certain of what they really said.

When it's your turn to take the witness stand, it's normal to be nervous. First comes the direct examination. Your attorney will ask you questions to buttress points made in the opening argument.

The opposing attorney's cross-examination follows, seeking to impeach your credibility. The other side's lawyer takes as departure points statements you made during the direct examination. Even if you were fairly confident when you entered the courtroom, it's not easy to maintain your composure. Whether the opposing counsel's style is blistering and caustic or smooth as silk, he or she has one purpose—to discredit what you say. Throughout the cross-examination the opposing counsel will endeavor to find contradictions, suggest alternative interpretations, or catch you off guard by bringing up something you didn't consider or even know. If the opposing attorney can shake you, your testimony loses value. After rattling your composure, the attorney may press you to reconsider, qualify, or possibly retract statements you made earlier.

No matter how you steel yourself, it's hard not to take the attack personally. If you become angry, flustered, or distracted, you will find it more difficult to recall facts and make your testimony compelling. Even people who are professionals in the courtroom feel at times that they're having the rug pulled out from under them. The difference is they don't take it personally. Try to ignore the tone of the attorney cross-examining you; focus instead on the substance of the question. If you have a momentary lapse in composure, all is not lost. Depending on the circumstances, you can turn to the judge and apologize—"I'm sorry, your Honor"—or simply regroup emotionally and go on.

Remember when you're testifying that, more than anyone else in the courtroom, you know what you have lived through. Having sworn to tell the truth and nothing but the truth, you must do your best to render accurate and compelling testimony. If you don't know the answer to a question, say so. If you are struggling to recall particular details, say that you are responding to the best of your recollection.

Having heard the opening statement of each attorney, a judge can pretty well anticipate what you and your spouse will say. Therefore, truthful witnesses can make or break a case. After all witnesses have testified, each attorney makes a summation or closing argument, asserting why his or her client should have custody, repeating his or her view of the case, and telling the court how the evidence has supported it while refuting the other attorney's position.

Imagine the task of the judge, who must digest the torrent of information. As witnesses testify hour after hour, in some cases day after day, the judge must remain attentive. I have seen judges make notes and type on small computers.

Judges vary as to how long they take to deliberate and rule on custody cases. In the cases in which I have testified, the final ruling usually has been made immediately after closing arguments by the attorneys. In several instances, judges have taken cases under advisement and did not issue a ruling for days or weeks. The longest that I have seen (in a court where I very seldom testify) was a judge taking close to a year to rule.

I have enormous respect for judges who preside over custody disputes. Not only are they legal experts but they are also sensitive to what parents are going through. In the instance of a parent representing himself because he cannot afford to hire a lawyer, I have seen judges bend over backwards to assist that parent so that he feels heard. The judges before whom I have testified appear genuinely to care about children and conscientiously to strive to do what truly is in the child's best interest.

Litigation

Once a judge has ruled on a custody case, you can either live with the consequences or find a way to appeal if circumstances warrant it. Some custody cases seem never to end because parents attempt to use litigation for their own purposes. Failing to get along, playing out their vendettas, they drag each other back to court over and over. After completing a custody evaluation and offering recommendations to the court, I was involved with one family's ongoing custody and visitation issues for seven years. The parents were filing motions to hold each other in contempt, seeking to change visitation, and making repeated attempts to alter the custody arrangements. All four children could have been sent to college on the money that was expended in these efforts.

Whereas parents can harass each other by filing various motions in court, it isn't easy to get into court to pursue a change once custody has been decided. There must be a change of circumstances for a judge to hear the case. Something major that will drastically affect the child's welfare must loom on the horizon or already have occurred.* Perhaps the child's environment is radically different because of a parent's remarriage, or a parent may no longer be able to care for a child adequately.

If one parent plans to move from the area and take the child, this definitely qualifies as a change in circumstances. In most jurisdictions the parent seeking to move must notify the other parent within a specified number of days. If the other parent contests the move, the court will hear the case. In some instances one parent just wants to move as far away from the other as possible. However, a parent cannot readily do this unless the circumstances are compelling. I recommended to one judge that a mother be allowed to move across the country with her two children not just because she had a wonderful job opportunity but mainly because the children's father had been abusive to all of them. Less contact with the father would give the mother a respite from harassment and spare all of them that stress and disruption. The judge did not stand in the way of the mother's move.

If the child has a good relationship with both parents, it is difficult to convince a court that such a move would be in the youngster's best interest. However, there are situations in which by moving

---

* The California Court of Appeal, Fourth Appellate District, ruled that "once there has been an initial judicial determination of custody, the trial court can change custody only if changed circumstances make such an order essential or expedient for the welfare of the child." Montenegro v. Diaz, No. EO25810, Cal. App. 4th, July 10, 2000, cited in *Matrimonial Strategist,* vol. 13, no. 7 (August 2000), p. 8.

a parent can improve the quality of his or her life and, arguably, that of the child. A parent may have a career opportunity that will allow for greater stability and improved financial circumstances. A parent may want to move to where there will be support from an extended family and an overall better quality of life. These cases are often very difficult for judges to decide.

IV

The Seven Deadly Errors Parents Make and How to Avoid Them

GOING THROUGH A DIVORCE is stressful even when your spouse is cooperative. The nightmarish situations I've described in the preceding sections are not inevitable. You can avoid them if you conscientiously try to think about your child first and foremost. This isn't always easy to do, though, because precisely at the time your youngster needs you, you may be worn out psychologically or physically or both.

Remember that, like it or not, through your child you remain connected forever to your spouse. You'll need to make decisions and plans long after your offspring reaches adulthood. Graduations, weddings, holidays, birthdays, and the sharing of grandchildren can be joyous or marred by conflict. Many children of divorced parents experience ongoing anxiety and guilt when they face choices that are likely to hurt one or the other parent. Consider the plight of a daughter who elopes because she can't bear the thought that she might offend one or both parents as she makes wedding plans and, in addition, dreads that the smoldering hostility between her mom and dad may erupt at her wedding. Then consider the far more desirable situation of a young woman joyfully anticipating her wedding day, confident that her divorced mom and dad will participate in the celebration without incident because they have remained cordial through the years.

When parents cooperate and think about their child first rather than about how to defeat each other, the child's losses are minimized and opportunities open up. Most important, the youngster feels secure in knowing that both parents love him or her, that there's no need to choose between them. Each supports the child's relationship with the other parent and remains interested and involved in all aspects of his or her life. Because Mom and Dad communicate, the child doesn't miss out on social functions, school activities, extracurricular events, or other special occasions.

When you are trying to resolve conflicts rather than win a war, you're not squandering your resources. Although you may still need an attorney to represent your interest in a divorce, you're not pouring money into unending litigation. The funds are available for other purposes, many of which will benefit your child.

You might ask, What if my spouse is a controller? Are parents who are controllers capable of abandoning their attempts to dominate in order to give priority to their child's welfare? Can people really change? In my career as a clinical psychologist, I have watched men and women make significant changes in lifelong habits when they had a personal crisis. Some sought professional help; others changed on their own. A major event that rocks the foundations of people's lives prompts them to evaluate what is really important.

I have seen parents who were minimally involved with their offspring turn over a new leaf. When the family was intact, the children were always there but the parent had other interests. As the marriage crumbled, the parent suddenly realized that he or she might lose a son or daughter. A new involvement may spring from a desire to get back at one's spouse and "win" custody, but as the parent sees the child flourish because of the attention, maintaining a good relationship becomes an end in itself. The parent genuinely becomes concerned and tries to do what is best for the youngster. Control is no longer the main motivator.

In this section I'll suggest what you can do to help your child survive and thrive through your divorce. I'll identify the seven most insidious errors that parents make as they separate and establish new lives. These errors, which can be devastating to your child's security and sense of well-being, can all be avoided. I'll also offer suggestions on how you can take a more positive approach. Despite the uncertainties and stress of a family breakup, you have within your power the ability and the moral obligation to do what truly is in the best interest of your child.

Error 1

Denigrating the Other Parent

EVEN IN THE most solid marriages, a child is likely to hear one parent comment negatively about the other. You might make such a remark directly to the child, to your spouse within earshot of your child, or even to other people in front of your child. As your marriage comes apart, tensions rise and differences are magnified, so you react more quickly and emotionally. Consequently, in unguarded moments you may make an ugly remark about your spouse to your child. Then another. Then another. What does this do to your child?

Children are resilient. From their own experience they know how people act when they are angry, hurt, or disappointed. They aren't destroyed by hearing one parent's occasional grumbling or raising his or her voice. For example, a mother and son are waiting for a father who is two hours late. Mom, exasperated, complains about how often Dad is late and remarks that he could have called rather than leave them sitting around. Listening to his mother vent her feelings does the child no harm. Most likely the youngster has similar thoughts. However, the effect on the child might be different were his mother to launch into a tirade about all the father's shortcomings and how his current thoughtlessness shows how selfish a human being he truly is.

There is a world of difference between complaining about a specific event and making pervasive, global criticisms aimed not just at your spouse's behavior but at his or her character. Attempts by one parent to denigrate the other may be sporadic or unrelenting and methodical. In either case they take a toll on a child. Can you imagine loving both your parents and then hearing from each how terrible the other is? You would feel sad, confused, and trapped. You would start doubting your own perceptions. What do you believe? Whom do you believe? If you believe one, how can you believe the other? How do you manage to love a parent the other hates? And what do you do with your anger as your parents continue tearing each other to pieces? You feel under pressure to take sides, but that's the last thing you want to do. This is a phenomenal burden of guilt to place on small shoulders, and it tears kids up inside.

I've found that the most disparaging remarks come from parents whose marriage has been shattered by a spouse's affair. There is nothing like the anger of a spouse who discovers that his or her partner has found someone else and wants out of the marriage. The shock, the sense of betrayal, the self-doubt, the outrage all make it difficult for a parent to feel, much less voice, anything positive about a spouse. Although most parents are able to control themselves enough not to mention the adultery in front of their child (I've seen many regrettable exceptions, though), their anger may permeate most of their interactions with the other parent and leak out in harsh criticisms in front of the child.

Many parents remain chronically angry as they face one hardship after another during divorce proceedings. Jack found that the salary from his regular job was insufficient to pay child support and keep up with his own living expenses. He'd had to move from a house to an apartment, then to a rented room with no telephone. Still he had to take an additional part-time job to avoid going into debt. He couldn't afford an automobile and had to rely on public transportation or his ex-wife's willingness to drive in order to spend time with his children. Jack detested his ex-wife and blamed her for his financial straits, so he did everything he could, including finding many ways to put her down in front of the children, to make her miserable. If the children were a few minutes late when he arrived, he yelled and pounded on his ex-wife's door. He wedged his body through the door to force her to respond to his complaints and accusations. When he returned the children he told her that they'd said they didn't want to spend time with her. Rather than hold a civil discussion, Jack barked orders, made snide remarks, and issued ultimatums, all in front of his children. This behavior convinced me that the co-parenting necessary for joint custody would be impossible for Jack. The mother obtained sole custody of the children, and Jack had visitation every other weekend and one evening during the week. His anger not only limited his custody options but left his children hurt and bewildered.

What a parent says or does in front of his or her child can range from mild criticism to a systematic campaign to tear down the other parent and assail all aspects of his or her life, including family, friends, work, and activities. The tactics are most extreme when one tries to alienate the child from the other parent and obliterate him or her from the other's life. This is precisely what Alice tried to do to Henry.

Because of a misunderstanding, Henry picked Doug up from

school and took him shopping on a day when Doug was supposed to have gone straight to his mother's house. Alice became frantic when Doug didn't arrive home at the regular time. She called the school and learned that he was with his father. When Henry dropped Doug off later, Alice treated her son as though he were a rescued hostage. Doug told me, "Mom was scared and said I was kidnapped." When I asked this six-year-old if he knew what the word meant, he replied, "Like somebody took you in their car and drove away, somebody you didn't know." Asked if he thought that this had happened to him, Doug replied, "No, but my mom did." I asked how he felt about the situation and he said, "Sad, because my mommy and daddy are fighting." Two years later nothing had changed; Doug told me, "It just makes me sad about the whole thing happening, that my dad's not talking to my mom."

After three years Alice's unrelenting denigration of her ex-husband had taken its toll. Henry lamented, "I've lost this child." When Henry attended his son's soccer games, Doug didn't even acknowledge his presence. Doug still spent time with his dad, often under protest, but refused to stay overnight at his home.

For years Henry had been on the horns of a dilemma. While he had defended himself against the most egregious of Alice's charges, overall he had been careful not to say anything negative to Doug about his mother. His restraint availed little against Alice's onslaught. Once she obtained sole custody, Alice was even less guarded in her remarks to Doug about his dad. Henry reported, "The whole picture is so skewed. [Alice] has the custodial care. I'm like a distant uncle." Actually, the boy's father was more disadvantaged in relating to Doug than an uncle might have been. "I walk around on eggshells," he commented and described how fearful he was that if he disappointed Doug in any way he'd complain to his mother and she would use it as ammunition to further undermine the father-son relationship.

Alice had been waging this war since Doug was in preschool. Living with his mom and dependent upon her after the separation, Doug gradually internalized what she told him. His mother was his sole protector—why would she lie to him? Gradually Alice took from Henry what was most precious to him—his son. Henry considered legal action. But he realized that no legal redress, if he could obtain any, would win over Doug's heart. In fact, it might alienate him further because if legal proceedings were pending Doug would be under even greater pressure from his mother to side with her.

In situations like this both parents and child lose something. The child gets put in the middle and feels compelled to make a choice. To be loyal to his mother, Doug had to reject his father. Alice lost in her ex-husband a valuable resource to help raise their son, especially as he approached the difficult adolescent years. Because of his occupation, Henry was a world traveler who had exceptional opportunities that would have been educational and exciting to Doug.

Henry had acted as a model of self-restraint. Trying his utmost to be the opposite of his ex-wife, he had refused to perpetuate a pattern of denigration. In the short run his refusal to fight back didn't seem to serve him well. However, Henry understood that if he had retaliated, Doug would have had no peace. The boy would have remained in the middle, confused and angry. By sacrificing the relationship he wanted, Henry was able to calm what otherwise would have been a continuing storm around the boy, giving him some tranquillity.

Sometimes the reverse occurs. A child has a strong relationship with one parent and the other parent's attempt to undermine it backfires. The parent who bad-mouths the other loses credibility in the child's eyes.

In some custody cases where abuse has been falsely alleged, the hypocrisy becomes obvious. One parent cries abuse while still allowing the child to spend hours alone with the other. Jim's wife warned that by the time she finished testifying in court he would be lucky ever to see their daughter. She threatened to provide the court with abundant evidence that Jim was an unfit parent. Meanwhile, she left their child alone in Jim's care for hours twice a week while she worked. The girl knew she wasn't being abused but resented her mom making life difficult for both her and her dad. She asked her father if they could leave and live together.

A parent's campaign to disparage the other can truly traumatize the child. At age twelve Thomas completely rejected his father, refusing even to speak with him by telephone. A year later he had a dramatic change of heart. Initially, Thomas declared to me, "I didn't have a decent childhood." He attributed this to "a lunatic dad, not playing with a full deck of cards." Characterizing his father as a tyrant, Thomas said that he was impatient, explosive, and mean. He also complained that his dad mistreated his mother. Thomas's mom was determined to cut her husband out of her life and the life of their son as completely and permanently as one would excise a malignant tumor. She commented that making Thomas spend time with his father was "like forcing people into a gulag."

I interviewed Thomas and his parents and talked to others who knew them all well. I could never come close to corroborating this diabolical picture of Thomas's dad. Having swallowed every aspect of his mother's denigration of his father, Thomas was mistreating his father more than the other way around. Thomas gave his father the silent treatment, accused him of abuse, and called his dad by his mother's boyfriend's first name. The evidence indicated that Thomas felt psychologically compelled to ally himself with his mother and renounce his father. He implored me, "Let me live without hassles; I hate it when I'm around him."

I believed, however, that there would be a significant psychological cost to Thomas shutting his father out of his life. To determine whether there was any foundation remaining on which to build a positive relationship, I proposed that Thomas and his dad meet with me. I will never forget watching Thomas shuffle down the walkway behind his father, looking as though he were being led to an execution chamber. When the two of them entered my office, Thomas positioned his chair so that he wouldn't have to face his dad. He would neither look at his father nor address him directly. He spoke only to me, and that was to complain vehemently about being forced to spend even this small amount of time in his father's presence.

Retaining his composure and not reacting directly to all that his son was dishing out, the father told his son how important he was to him and how saddened he was by the boy's attitude. When the meeting ended Thomas darted out the door and ran ahead of his father. Although the judge found the father fit to be a custodial parent, she gave sole custody to the mother and said that, given Thomas's age, she didn't think it wise or practical to compel him to visit his father. She left Thomas with the option to exercise visitation if he changed his mind. There seemed to be no hope for resuscitation of a father-son relationship.

But two years later I ran into Thomas's dad and asked him how things were. He was delighted to report that Thomas had changed his mind. He had wearied of the constant bickering between his mom and his new stepdad. Thomas asked to live with his father, and his mother agreed to relinquish custody.

A child who remains angry about the family splitting up may find a convenient scapegoat for that anger—the parent who is vilified the most. Two years after the separation, even though he continued to complain bitterly about his father, Doug told me that if he could have three wishes, his first still would be "that my parents were married." I have always believed that Doug actually was angry at both parents for shattering his world by separating. In only the most concrete way do young children understand why their parents have stopped living together. They'll explain to me that there was too much yelling, or Daddy had to work too much. It is easier to piece everything together if there is a good guy and a bad guy. Hearing one parent vilify the other helps a child make sense of the incomprehensible. At the same time, the vilification has the potential to damage a previously positive parent-child relationship.

Six-year-old Katie was struggling to understand why her parents separated. Katie's mother was convinced that her husband was an alcoholic. However, she had only a malicious motive for expressing her views on this subject to Katie. During one interview Katie told me that she was scared of her dad. When I asked why, she replied, "I forgot why." Earlier she had remarked that her father had been drinking a bottle of beer. I asked her if this had anything to do with her being frightened. This six-year-old replied, "I'm afraid he'd get drunk." When I asked what this meant, she said, "I don't know what that means." I asked her where she had heard about getting drunk. Katie responded, "I don't know. My mommy said that." After this exchange she enthusiastically described playing with her father.

I am not disputing the mother's right to be concerned about her husband's drinking. One could argue that she would be derelict in her duty as a parent if she ignored alcohol consumption that might jeopardize Katie. However, confusing and scaring her daughter showed an inability to separate her own issues from what was in Katie's best interest.

During his or her parents' separation, the child already has suffered one loss—the loss of the family unit. What crueler thing can one parent do than to inflict another loss by attempting to sabotage the positive relationship that child has always had with the other parent!

Correction: Bury Your Anger and Help Your Child Maintain a Positive Relationship with Both Parents

Having been married for years, you know your spouse's personality and habits. You've seen how he or she reacts to frustration and disappointment. As you divorce, you're not dealing with a stranger. You should know what to expect, not in every instance but generally. Showing your anger won't change your spouse.

Anger is wasteful and destructive. Although you may feel charged up when angry, anger drains energy from problem solving. Your energy is finite; why spend it being counterproductive? Also, anger interferes with clear thinking, so you're less likely to make sound decisions when angry. Expressing anger may temporarily intimidate the other person into doing what you want, but it's more likely to alienate him or her and provoke more anger.

Anger arises when there's a gap between expectations and reality. If a pen writes in blue, you would not expect it to write in red, no matter what you did. The pen is as it is. The same is true with your spouse or ex-spouse. Of course, a person has the capacity to change, but if the other parent was habitually late when you were married, he or she is likely to continue to be late. Instead of getting incensed at his or her lack of punctuality, make use of this knowledge. When possible, build extra time into the schedule that allows for lateness. If that isn't feasible and the problem persists, remember that venting your anger will only exacerbate the conflict and make your child more unhappy.

If the other parent hoards papers from school instead of passing them on to you, polite but firm reminders may help. Anger will not. Instead of expecting blood from a stone, find a way to circumvent the obstacle. For example, tell the appropriate school personnel about the problem and supply self-addressed, stamped envelopes so that information can be sent directly to you. Develop a relationship with the teacher so he or she appreciates the problem and works with you to address it. Create schedules and reminders—one for the other parent's home, one for yours, and one for the child's backpack—to avoid confusing situations that spark anger.

I am not suggesting that you become a doormat. Assertiveness and a calm demeanor are not incompatible. Your spouse is far more likely to listen when you're polite than when you're belligerent and demanding.

Anger also results when you think you're losing control. Men and women who pursue power and control as ends in themselves frequently get angry because the control they seek eludes them. However, the expectation that you can control another adult human being is unrealistic. Becoming angry because you cannot control your spouse or ex-spouse is an exercise in futility.

You probably know at least one person who almost never gets angry. Whatever the frustration or disappointment, he or she takes life in stride. That serenity is the result of accepting, however reluctantly, what he or she cannot control and trying to make the best of the situation. Many of these parents tell me they live by the Serenity Prayer:

> God grant me the serenity to accept the things I cannot change, the courage to change the things I can, and the wisdom to know the difference.

Anger also results when you feel put down, personally attacked, or dismissed. However, the sense of being put down exists only in the mind of the recipient. As Eleanor Roosevelt said, "No one can make you feel inferior without your consent." Consider the nature of a put-down. It is one person's attempt to build himself up by diminishing another. If you're on the receiving end, take a deep breath and think about what's being said. If the criticism has merit, accept and learn from it, even if the tone is harsh. If it doesn't apply, note the source and forget it.

People who are controllers readily feel put down because, to a considerable degree, their self-esteem relies on controlling others. Whenever someone disregards, disagrees with, or otherwise displeases them, even in a minor way, they feel totally deflated and react accordingly. Imagine pricking an inflated balloon with a pin; the whole thing bursts. Often controllers think in black-and-white terms. Either they prevail in a situation or they see themselves as completely powerless. Rather than tolerate being reduced to a zero, they respond angrily to show that they are to be reckoned with.

The case of Anita and Bill exemplifies how to remain calm while coping with a controlling bully. Bill was irate, not only because Anita had left him and taken the children but also because he had been cut adrift by his own family, whose patience and endurance were exhausted. Anita demonstrated remarkable equanimity in the face of Bill's unrelenting attempts to control her, even after three years of separation. E-mail correspondence between the two offers evidence of different personalities, one an ardent controller, the other a problem solver. Here is a typical exchange:

> **Anita:** *I don't see that writing letters and e-mails back and forth is moving us toward an agreement. Why don't I try to call you? Since you don't want me to call you at work, why don't you give me your number at home? I asked for it over a month ago.*
>
> **Bill:** *You must realize that I am a very important person in [the children's] lives. I am their father. I take very good care of them. . . . I have shown I am a good father, that I am a good example for them, and the court will realize that. . . . I see that we will be going to court over many issues due to your refusal to see my rights. Fine, let's get it over with.*

In another brief e-mail Anita requested Bill's new home address and phone number. Bill flew into a rage while Anita remained calm. After finally providing his home address and phone number, Bill launched an attack. In a three-page diatribe he proclaimed what a good father he had been, accused Anita of physically abusing the children, and threatened her with litigation. (There never was any finding that she had abused the children.)

Accustomed to Bill's harangues, Anita retained her composure. She knew that responding angrily would only fuel *his* anger and compound their problems. A cynic might say that Anita was restraining herself just to look good during the custody evaluation. Part of my job required finding out how she had functioned before such an evaluation had been contemplated. I found ample evidence that she was not the rigid, angry woman depicted by her husband. Two years before the custody battle began, Anita had written Bill to suggest they consult a mediator. Again, her tone says a lot about her and provides a model of effective communication:

> I'm writing to ask you to consider talking to someone in a mediating role, someone who might be able to facilitate some dialogue between us. . . . It's for the sake of having a less difficult divorce, and for the sake of us both being parents of the children in as good a way as possible that I'm proposing this.

With the letter Anita enclosed a check made payable to the mediator so that Bill could first meet with him alone without cost. He spurned her offer.

With seemingly little effort Anita remained calm even in extremely exasperating situations. Bill would castigate her in front of the children, making statements like "You're dumber than dog crap." She would remove herself from the scene as quickly as possible, saying only what was absolutely necessary. Anita's pastor referred to her as "a calming influence" in the children's lives. A therapist who counseled Anita on divorce-related matters praised her problem-solving orientation.

What was the advantage of Anita remaining calm and thinking clearly? Didn't her husband continue to push her around? Bill didn't change, so what good did her restraint do? She had methodically taken steps that enabled her to protect her children. She was the one who had asked the court for the custody evaluation, and the court adopted recommendations from the evaluation. She got sole custody of the children, while Bill's visitation time was limited. Because she had evidence of Bill's harshness in the face of her calm demeanor, arrangements for pickups and drop-offs of the children changed so that they occurred only in a public place, not at Anita's front door. This spared the children the turmoil they had been experiencing twice a week for nearly two years. A person with a more volatile personality might have responded angrily, which would have only vindicated and inflamed a person with Bill's type of personality.

You can take giant strides toward reducing anger by making up your mind to maintain a businesslike relationship with your spouse or ex-spouse. Your business is acting in the best interest of your child. To do this, you will need to let a lot go rather than take it personally. When your spouse makes a nasty comment or erupts in a temper tantrum, restrain yourself. Attend to the information, but let the nastiness blow by. A businesslike relationship calls for civility, thinking before reacting, then focusing on the issue.

Eliminating anger toward your spouse has a ripple effect. You are less burdened by negative thoughts and liberated from consuming anger. You can be more resourceful in seeking constructive solutions to problems. Although you have no control over how your spouse or ex-spouse will deal with a situation, by conducting yourself in a businesslike manner you are helping your child. He or she will be spared exposure to your anger. To the extent that the other parent takes a cue from you, your youngster benefits even more. If both parents turn down the heat and try to be civil, the child will be relieved from the stress of being in the cross fire. Feeling less compelled to side with either parent, your child will enjoy a better relationship with both of you.

During the year that I participated as an evaluator in Karen's custody case, I had known her to quarrel constantly with Blake, from whom she had separated. She complained that he neglected their baby's hygiene, ignored her medical needs, and was impervious to issues related to the infant's emotional well-being. Blake handed me an entire notebook documenting Karen's criticisms and the intermittent involvement of lawyers in resolving their differences. He despaired that Karen ever would credit him with doing anything right. The final divorce decree mandated that the couple meet with me yearly to assess "the child's custody and visitation schedule in relation to the child's development and her changing needs." I braced myself for the first of these post-divorce meetings, expecting an hour of bickering or worse. I was stunned to hear Karen and Blake having a civil conversation in the waiting room. To my astonishment, the two parents were in synch about the major issues. Karen indicated that she and Blake had recently had a power struggle over particular visitation days but that they had worked out their differences. These two people had grown weary of wasting time and energy arguing, as well as incurring the expense of involving lawyers in their fights. They discovered the merit of solving problems rather than continuing to accuse each other of sinister motives and incompetent parenting.

To help implement these suggestions, consider the following:

- As you are about to have contact with your spouse, ask yourself, What do I expect? Then question whether your expectation is realistic.
- After the fact, if you are angry ask yourself whether the anger arose from an unrealistic expectation.
- Try to distinguish between what you can and cannot control, understanding that you may have to swallow hard and accept a great deal of the latter.
- If you feel put down, ask yourself if you are personalizing something you need to let go of.
- Remember that anger gets in the way of solving problems.
- Focus on the issue, not on the person. Maintain a businesslike attitude.

Error 2

Communicating Poorly

IN MANY MARRIAGES that end in divorce, neither parent knows or cares much about what the other is thinking, feeling, or doing from day to day. Silence, avoidance, and bickering erode communication so that even essential information doesn't get transmitted.

During custody fights, parents often use the very instruments designed to facilitate communication to prevent it. Telephone, fax, mail, and e-mail become weapons by which divorcing parents further mean-spirited agendas. I have seen warring parents deploy the following tactics:

1. Hang up upon hearing the other parent's voice
2. Use the answering machine to screen calls, then decide whether to respond
3. Use caller ID to screen calls
4. Refuse to return calls or respond to other forms of communication
5. Leave terse, nasty messages on answering machines

6. Send letters, e-mails, or faxes that are accusatory and inflammatory
7. Falsely claim not to have received a letter, fax, e-mail, or phone message
8. Send letters return receipt requested, which requires the recipient to sign for the mail (proving that he or she received it) or, if he or she isn't home, to make a special trip to the post office

The following e-mail from a husband to his wife during a custody dispute shows mounting frustration as each party feels the other is thwarting communication.

I sent you a simple memo requesting to trade visitation dates. . . . You waited 9 days and eventually replied. . . . A simple no would have sufficed. Instead, you sent back your typical self-serving rhetoric where you ramble on about all sorts of issues, of course none true. . . . You always want to reduce things to some sort of B.S. battle hoping someone might one day believe you. And once again I seem compelled to defend the truth and reply.

These two people did no better by phone. For years each blasted the other for obstructionism. The mother wrote me a letter of frustration over the situation:

This business with [the father] denying my phone access to the children must be put to a stop. . . . I understand he is getting his revenge by not allowing my access by phone. No one really cares about that, but now he is preventing [my son's] access to me. . . .

Enough is enough! I have left many messages . . . without getting return calls. . . . [The child's father] will have to find another way to be vengeful to me.

The father charged that the mother was equally vengeful because she habitually left the phone off the hook or immediately activated her voice mail. The father later reported that his ex-wife deactivated the voice mail function so her phone rang continuously whenever he tried to call while his son was visiting.

Two controllers like these may go at each other indefinitely. However, a parent who is primarily a problem solver eventually may retreat from such nerve-racking hostile interchanges with a controller who seems to delight in precipitating confrontations. Annie explained why she found it so hard during their marriage to deal with her husband, Scott: "It's a personality thing. . . . To control me . . . he'd get in my face with his fingers pointed and tear into one thing or another." Annie later regretted that she did not stand up to her husband while they were married.

Once she separated from Scott, Annie wanted as little to do with him as possible. She sent him a letter suggesting they "send all future correspondence through our lawyers until things calm down." Accordingly, an order was entered in the court: "All communications between the parties shall occur between the parties' counsel except for emergency situations involving the child." This meant that resolving even the most trivial matter could cost hundreds of dollars. One parent would contact his or her attorney. That attorney would then communicate the issue, usually in writing (for the record) to the other attorney. Days or even weeks elapsed just to resolve the simplest issue.

Although Annie felt relieved about not having to deal personally with Scott, there were times when she wanted to pick up the
phone to ask him something directly. Realizing that perhaps she had
overreacted, Annie asked her lawyer to have the order rescinded,
which he did. There are cases, however, in which a parent's standard
and only response to his or her spouse is, "Talk to your lawyer and
have him talk to mine."

When communication breaks down, your child is likely to
become the message bearer. This can also complicate the transmis-
sion of straightforward information. The youngster may forget, mis-
understand, or confuse some aspect of the communication. If she
forgets to relay information that should have been taken care of by
her parents, the child may perceive herself as the cause of the argument that erupts between her mom and dad. She may become upset
when the information that she has conscientiously conveyed is dismissed by the recipient as unimportant. The communication delivered by the child may be important but appropriate only for adults
to handle. Innocently transmitting a support check or legal document, the youngster may find herself on the receiving end of a harsh
comment. She may conclude that her parent is angry at her for
doing something wrong whereas the anger is actually at the other
parent.

If you fail to communicate basic information, such as activity
schedules or a school calendar, you may not get to see your child's
play, soccer game, or music recital. Your child might also miss out on
attending his own event. These unfortunate situations occur when
mothers and fathers are so possessive and self-centered that they
behave as though they own the child. They don't communicate because they have no intention of including the other parent. And if

they don't want to attend the scheduled activity, they cavalierly assume the child can readily forgo it as well. They figure the time with their child is their time, and they'll decide what to do with it. The primary loser is the child, who wants to go on with his life and regular activities, and to have both his parents attend or participate in whatever he does.

An exception occurs when the parents behave so badly in the presence of each other that the child wants only one parent there. I have talked with boys and girls who dread what might transpire if both parents were to attend the same event, or if one parent showed up with someone the other detested, such as a boyfriend or girlfriend.

The emotional toll on your child of your failure to communicate is incalculable. Think of your child's plight witnessing the two people who matter most to him hating each other to the point that they will not speak. Sixteen-year-old Patrick was fed up. Since he was nine years old his parents had fought over custody. The last time they had gone to court he had told me that, more than anything, he wanted his mom and dad to talk to each other. Much to Patrick's disgust, they were at it again, gearing up for litigation. Still they weren't talking to each other: "I said whoever loses would be back at it again. It can only go on two more years. Then I'll have my own house. They can fight over who wants to pay for it. . . . Last time, I really emphasized I want them to start talking. If they don't do it, I want a punishment for them, like to sit in a locked room for two days and get no food if they don't talk or have their air supply shut off until they talk." This vivid expression of anger and frustration deserves to be taken seriously.

Correction: Put Yourself in Your Child's Shoes

Relieved to be on your own and liberated from day-to-day strife with your spouse, you probably don't want to think about, much less communicate with, him or her. However, your child may have a completely different perspective. As you contemplate having a divorce party with a cake and champagne to celebrate your freedom, your child may be fantasizing about your reconciling with your spouse. While you relish your independence, your child may be desperately hoping for a reconciliation.

Children are distressed when their parents don't communicate, whether they are still married, separated, or divorced. If you try to understand what your child is going through, you'll keep hearing that he or she wants you to talk to the other parent.

If you can't communicate directly and effectively with your spouse or ex-spouse, the best approach to facilitating communication is to empathize with your child. You can help your youngster in many ways if you're in tune with his or her feelings and view of the world (even if you don't agree with that view). If you empathize with your child, your cooperation with your ex-spouse almost has to improve because you'll realize how badly your child really wants and needs it.

Before you can empathize, you must listen. Being a good listener is difficult when you're tired and stress-ridden. It requires setting aside your own preoccupations and attending closely to what your child is saying as well as remaining sensitive to what he or she isn't telling you. Listening requires patience when your patience is in short supply. No matter how harried you are, take advantage of every opportunity to talk with your child. Listen to what your child says about how important it is to him or her for you and your ex-spouse to be civil and communicate with each other.

How you talk to your child about his or her relationship with your ex-spouse is crucial. Word choice matters a lot; it's more than just semantics. Consider how one parent refers to the time the child spends with the other. *Visitation* is a rather formal word, used by lawyers and courts. Usually a child doesn't "visit" a parent the way he "visits" a friend. He spends time with the parent on a regular basis. There is a difference in how it sounds to both your child and the other parent if you refer to visitation versus "spending time" together. If you adopt the formal language of the court, you're inviting your child into a world where he or she has no place, a world your child finds threatening, stressful, or terrifying. Choose your words wisely and kindly.

Some parents fail to empathize with a child because they're using the youngster to meet their own needs for a personal confidant, buddy, or therapist. Mothers and fathers may confuse being open and informative with dumping emotional problems onto their children. If you're dumping on your child, you're truly neglecting his or her needs. Unable to resolve parental problems, your youngster is left feeling more upset and helpless than ever. Avoid spilling your guts to your child about your private worries. Rather than impose on your child, seek out a friend or counselor who will listen and help.

While establishing your own schedule and routine, think of your child first, not as an afterthought. The more empathic you seem to your child, the more she will tell you. The more she tells you, the more you can help. I described earlier how children missed events and activities that were important to them because their parents were so self-absorbed that they failed to communicate with each other. Don't let vital matters slip through the cracks because you weren't paying attention and then failed to talk to the other parent.

A child benefits in many ways when a parent is trying to see things from his or her point of view. An empathic parent realizes that attention to details matters. Being sure your child has an adequate breakfast may seem like a small thing, especially with all the pressures of readying yourselves for school or work. I cannot tell you how many children have told me that they ate nothing for breakfast or grabbed a doughnut as they dashed out the door. You don't have to prepare an elaborate meal. But feeding your child properly shows that you are thinking about him. Remembering to sign a permission slip for a field trip, arranging teacher conferences, having his soccer uniform washed, arranging a ride so he can attend his afternoon softball practice, making play dates, giving him lunch money all indicate that each day you are thinking about what he needs. Recognizing and acknowledging your child's needs is half the battle, but you can't do everything by yourself. With an open channel of communication to your spouse, you can enlist help meeting the demands of your child's schedule, assistance caring for him if you have to be away, or get a breather if you just need some downtime.

When you're establishing a new home, think carefully about your child's needs, including access to the other parent. In choosing where to live, consider more than your own preferences. Think, if you were your child, what would you want? A safe neighborhood, other children nearby, closeness to school, the availability of recreational activities all might be important. Consider the advantages in terms of communication and logistics of living near the other parent.

In my work, I have seen many parents conscientiously try to put themselves in the place of their children. I witnessed a particularly valiant effort when a father abandoned pursuing custody of his two sons even though he was certain that he could mount a successful court case. After his wife took off to be with her lover nearly twelve hundred miles away, a court gave Mort custody of Ted and Donald. His now ex-wife married her paramour and continued to live out of state. Ted and Donald spent the entire summer and alternate holidays with their mother. Mort accommodated his ex-wife so that she could visit the children any time she wanted to, which she did on the average of once a month. Every time their mother had sought physical and legal custody of the boys, she'd lost in court.

Ted and Donald loved going to the beach and enjoyed the laissez-faire atmosphere of their mother's home. In contrast to that relaxed environment, the father required the boys to toe the line, establish priorities, and fulfill obligations. With interests in school, sports, and music, the children were faring quite well living with their father. Still, having lived with their dad for years, the boys, now ages nine and twelve, said they missed their mother and asked for the chance to live with her.

Mort told me that, based on his ex-wife's instability and attempts to alienate the boys from him, he believed he could retain custody. The question he pondered was whether he might win that battle but "lose the hearts" of his sons. As he put it, "So I win the court battle, and the kids hate me." He nonetheless worried about the "undefined risk" in a change of custody. Donald and Ted would live not only with their mother and a stepdad but also with two stepbrothers, whom they did not know all that well. How would they do living together full-time? Proud of his boys, Mort told me, "I couldn't be happier; they're growing up to be well-adjusted young men." He worried about whether their development would be nurtured by a mother whom Mort knew did not fully share his values.

Mort considered moving to his ex-wife's neighborhood so he could maintain a close watch and sustain his relationship with his sons, but he wasn't sure he could manage this financially. Furthermore, if he moved Donald and Ted would find it difficult to visit their many friends. Much of their life would just disappear.

After wavering for a time, critically examining his own motives and questioning himself about what was best for his sons, Mort decided to sign a consent order giving his ex-wife custody. This sacrifice spared everyone thousands of dollars in legal expenses and the emotional bruising of yet another court proceeding, and it enhanced the potential for improving communication with his ex-wife, something Donald and Ted had long wanted.

To communicate civilly and productively with the other parent, consider the following:

- As you put yourself in the place of your child, think about how important the other parent is to him or her.
- Set aside your antipathy toward your ex-spouse so you can communicate for the benefit of your child.
- Remember that communication with your ex-spouse is vital to

your child's stability. If you fail to communicate, your child may miss important events and opportunities.

- Find the most emotionally neutral way to transmit information and exchange views.
- Listen to your child so you don't lose sight of what's important to him or her or how your behavior might be hurtful.

Error 3

Making Your Child Compartmentalize His or Her Life

IF YOU AND your spouse share custody, even in the best of circumstances your child has a huge adjustment to make living in two homes rather than one. Invariably he or she will encounter differences, some of them major, in daily routine, in each parent's expectations, in the rules that are set, and in the discipline that is administered. Your child will probably have to get used to at least one new neighborhood, perhaps a new school, and making new friends.

Cooperative parents strive for continuity and help their children cope. When animosity is intense, your child will have to live in two usually very different worlds or war zones, which must be kept separate. The walls go up about what can and cannot be discussed freely with one parent regarding what goes on when the child is with the other. There are two reasons why parents—often unthinkingly—subject their offspring to this sort of pressure. As separated parents establish new lives, they want to maintain a degree of privacy, and they feel freer if the ex-spouse knows as little as possible about what they're doing. The pressures for secrecy are especially strong when the parents despise each other. It then becomes a great emotional burden for a child to act with each parent as though life with the other does not exist.

Children are under the greatest pressure to compartmentalize their lives when both parents are controllers aiming to eliminate each other from their child's life. These men and women genuinely believe that they are good parents. They satisfy the material needs of their youngster, foster participation in activities, and spend considerable time talking, reading, and playing with him or her, but each refuses to acknowledge that the other parent can contribute anything worthwhile to the child's life. They may even regard aspects of that parent's life as toxic influences. If only one parent is a controller, the youngster still feels pressure to compartmentalize life. When he or she is with the controlling parent, the child dares not say much about the other unless it is negative. When he or she is with the more reasonable parent, the child is reluctant to say much about the controller for fear that somehow the latter will find out and become angry.

Compartmentalization is a self-protective measure for the child. In one family in which the parents had separated, the father regarded the mother as mentally ill, emotionally unstable, and overly permissive. The mother viewed her ex-spouse as running his home like the military to serve his own needs but oblivious to their daughter's needs. The parents no longer had any direct communication. They exchanged their daughter at a neutral place without speaking. They did not talk by telephone. Although e-mail could have been an efficient means of transmitting helpful information, the parents used it instead to berate each other. Knowing that her parents detested each other, the girl understandably disclosed very little when speaking with one about the other. To protect herself, she tried even to avoid thinking about her mom while she was with her dad and vice versa. She lived as though the court had imposed a gag order on her; and she suffered emotionally for it.

I have seen instances in which efforts by a controller to force a child to compartmentalize his life backfire. Strong-willed about many things at age eleven, Donna was emphatic about whom she wanted to live with: "I don't want my dad to get custody. . . . I'd probably cry every day. I wouldn't eat because I'd be so depressed." Donna told me that her father instructed her, "Don't say anything to your mom about here. What goes on here is here, and there is there." Her mother was the opposite, an open person who made no such demands. Bristling with resentment, Donna declared, "I have a right to tell my mom what goes on. I tell him what goes on. He sits right there listening to what I have to say. Everywhere we go, he goes unless we have to go to the bathroom." Donna complained that she couldn't even call her mother without her dad eavesdropping. Ultimately she was able to escape her father's tyranny when a judge ordered supervised visitation and her mother was given sole custody.

Most children don't have a parent as insensitive as Donna's father, so they don't strongly prefer one parent over another. They love both parents, are loyal to both and, most of all, want to please both. It's painful and confusing for the child if one parent's pleasure is the other's displeasure. One nine-year-old told me about the pressure she was feeling during the custody litigation: "It's like choosing one parent, like you love one more than the other. I love both, and I'd like to see them just as much." Not only did she want to spend time with both parents but she also wanted them to have a decent relationship with each other so that she didn't have to hide from one what she was doing with the other.

A psychologist described seven-year-old Benjamin as searching for "islands of safety" while he was forced to compartmentalize his existence not only with either parent but with his psychotherapist, his school, extracurricular activities, and even his laughter. In a later memorandum, the psychologist warned that Benjamin "now finds himself in a situation where his development is indeed being pretty seriously abused."

Neal, Benjamin's father, took sharp issue with the psychologist's assessment. He was adamant that his son didn't need therapy. Many people say they don't "believe" in psychotherapy, so Neal's opinion was not unusual. In this case, however, a court order supported therapy. Rather than encourage his son to participate and benefit, this father subverted the process by telling his son he opposed it and by never taking him to a session. (It was always his mother, Lucy, who brought Benjamin because she believed he needed help.) Except for saying, "My father doesn't want me to come here," Benjamin volunteered almost nothing about his dad or about what he did when he spent time with him. After I had established rapport with this boy, he confided that his dad had told him not to discuss him during our meetings.

Lucy paid Benjamin's school tuition. Proclaiming that Benjamin's "education comes from me," his father contended that the school was too easy for his son and refused to pay a penny to the institution. Neal refused to attend school conferences or any other event at which Lucy would be present. He ignored his ex-wife's written instructions about Benjamin's dietary restrictions. He refused to take Benjamin to sports activities in which his mother had enrolled him. He asserted that, because he was living with his mother, Benjamin had no friends, a charge I found to be without foundation. Neal insisted that Benjamin's time with his mother be cut back until she straightened herself out.

Despite being on the receiving end of such intense hatred, Lucy didn't respond in kind. She acknowledged that her ex-husband "can be such a terrific father; he has good qualities." She often expressed her desire for a better relationship, not because she cared about her ex-husband but because she couldn't bear to see her son suffering. She was saddened by seeing Benjamin freeze emotionally when his two worlds threatened to overlap. For example, Lucy recalled that her son had admonished her "no more laughing" just before his father came to pick him up. He was terrified that his dad might arrive and see him and his mom having fun together. Whenever the phone rang, Benjamin instructed his mother to turn down the radio or television so his father wouldn't think other people were present.

Over time Benjamin began to trust me and confided more. He said that he got stomachaches "all the time." He wanted to play basketball but his father disapproved. On one occasion Benjamin told me that to avoid having to choose between playing in a game and doing what his father wanted, "I might make myself not feel good." Eventually he chose not to participate at all. Benjamin couldn't understand why his father disliked his school so much. As Benjamin improved academically and got along better, he became increasingly positive about school. However, his joy in winning a scholastic award was sharply diminished because he thought his father might be angry since he hated the school so much.

Benjamin developed an attachment to his mother's boyfriend, who was very good to him. Not only did he have to hide how he felt from his father but he sensed he was being disloyal. His father called the man names, instructed Benjamin not to go anywhere with him, and told him not to be nice to him. Benjamin was puzzled and angry. "He always says he hates him. That's crazy. He doesn't even know him. How can you hate someone if you don't know him? You don't know what they're like. . . . For a while I didn't want anything to do with him because [Daddy] didn't like him. But I do now!"

Although Benjamin was repeatedly given the message by his father that everything about his mother and her life was poison, he remained deeply attached to both parents and enjoyed his time with each. Neal immersed his son in a world of books, cultural activities, and foreign travel. It was not just that he spent money on his son; Neal also spent enormous amounts of time with him and truly cared about him. But he completely failed to recognize that Benjamin's enjoyment of life with his mother did not detract from their relationship.

Benjamin had two parents who loved him. Tragically he was emotionally tied in knots while struggling to keep both worlds separate. He remarked that each parent told him different things, so he didn't know whom to believe. You can imagine how frustrated and angry he was. No custody arrangement can significantly lighten the psychological burden of compartmentalization in a situation like Benjamin's. The court ordered that he reside primarily with his mother and have liberal visitation with his father. A year later, after another court hearing, I heard that the parents were getting tired of the expensive court battles and getting along somewhat better.

A child who compartmentalizes his life must constantly watch himself. He is apprehensive whenever there is the prospect of the two worlds coming together. As Benjamin's previous evaluator phrased it, he was "nervously triple-guessing" himself. Under such circumstances a child may develop intense fear and guilt even by thinking about one parent while in the presence of the other. When a child is continually forced to compartmentalize his life, the potential for developing serious psychological disorders, psychosomatic symptoms, and physical illness is enormous.

The consequences for a child living an existence like Benjamin's can even be life-threatening. Think of what might happen if a child is seriously injured during an athletic event. One parent isn't available, and the coach cannot reach the other because his or her name was deliberately left off the emergency contact form. Someone other than a parent might have to make a life-or-death decision about the child.

Correction: Support Your Child's Relationship with the Other Parent

No child should have a "parentectomy" because of a divorce. Your child has lost the family unit, don't let him or her lose a parent too. It's in a youngster's best interest to maintain a relationship with both Mom and Dad without feeling pressured to take sides.

If your child wants to do something with the other parent, this isn't to say that he or she loves you less. Even before you separated your child chose to do certain things more with one parent than the other. Only a very thin-skinned parent feels slighted or diminished by a child's preferences. Your child should be able to confide in either or both of you without negative repercussions.

Never assume that your child thinks the way you do about your ex-spouse. Lois characterized her husband, Frank, as so intimidating that she feared for her physical safety. Claiming that she had suffered emotional and physical abuse, Lois worried about the safety of their seven-year-old daughter, Mary. But Mary didn't seem at all afraid. Rather she always spoke of having a fun time with her dad, playing in a fort, flying a kite, and tossing a Frisbee. Asked if she wished for anything to be different in her life, Mary replied without hesitating, "Mom and Dad living with each other in the same place, and one staying home and one working." Amy, her four-year-old sister, expressed similar sentiments. Asked what she wished for more than anything in the world, Amy exclaimed, "My daddy!" Asked why, her response was simply, "Because I love him."

I believed that Lois had some legitimate, although exaggerated, concerns about her husband. The challenge for her was to bear in mind that, whatever Frank's flaws, he remained the children's father, and they adored him. Mary and Amy should have been able to enjoy their father without their mother's apprehensions intruding. Lois began to separate her problems with Frank from the relationship he had with the girls. She realized if they constantly encountered her negativism, they would be apt to clam up and treat their experiences with their dad as an entirely separate life. If the girls compartmentalized their lives in this fashion, Lois feared that the flow of information would be turned off like a water spigot. If difficulties arose, she would be far less likely to hear about them than if she supported the girls' relationship with their father. Thinking about all this, Lois changed her approach and showed a positive interest in the girls' activities with their dad. Mary and Amy were delighted to be able to come home and talk freely about their visits.

Sometimes one parent's continued trashing of the other pushes a child in an unanticipated direction. Ten-year-old Brad complained that his mother was telling him things he didn't want to hear, especially about his father's debts and failure in business; he noticed that before his parents separated, he didn't have to hear about such matters. Brad told me, "I'd like to see my dad a little more often." On a psychological test that assesses how a child perceives his parents, Brad rated his father higher on three times as many items as he did his mother.

Brad was fighting as hard as he could to preserve a life with both parents. He didn't want to be pressed into choosing between them. Without my asking for a preference, Brad announced that he wanted to spend a week at each house, alternating time with his mom and dad. He resisted compartmentalization.

Brad's mother finally got it, but her son was the one teaching her the lesson. Her not-so-subtle denigration of his father was pushing Brad closer to him, not further from him. She began to see that Brad's self-confidence was boosted by his dad's encouraging him in athletics and attending every game and practice. Brad's mom began practicing self-restraint before making a disparaging remark about her ex-spouse and forcing her son to wall off both sides of his world.

Alarmed by their daughter's behavior, two other divorced parents altered their pattern of interaction. Eleven-year-old Esther became defiant and physically aggressive toward her mother. She refused to comply with her mom's requests, screamed "I hate you," and slapped her mother. Mother and daughter often became embroiled in what could best be called a power contest. Esther's dad, who spent less time with her than the mother, reported no such problems. This was a perfect opportunity for the father to rub salt in the wounds inflicted during the divorce, for he had contended in a fiercely fought custody battle that the mother was volatile and unstable and predicted she would have problems with Esther. In fact, he took no satisfaction in what was going on and was as troubled as his ex-wife.

Esther's mother called and said that both she and her ex-husband would meet with me. Having last seen these two parents during the custody war, I witnessed something a year later that I never would have envisioned. Mom and Dad came to focus on a problem rather than each other. Instead of finger-pointing, a cooperative attitude prevailed. Both parents had decided to be problem solvers.

These parents assured me that, despite their differences with each other, they were a "united front" when it came to Esther. They wanted their daughter to know that they would work cooperatively, perhaps far better than they did when they all lived together, so her life would not be compartmentalized. Just the opposite! Esther would experience a smoother, well-integrated existence as she spent time with each parent.

Like Brad and Esther, children of divorce need the opportunity to live one well-integrated life, not a fractured existence in which they wall off alternating halves of their lives in order to get along with each parent. To encourage your child's relationship with the other parent:

• Don't assume that your child shares your view of the other parent.

- Encourage your child to discuss freely what he or she does with the other parent.
- Beware of the fine line between asking and grilling. Your motive should be to encourage your child to enjoy time with the other parent, not invade your ex's privacy.
- Listen carefully to your child's comments so you have a better understanding of his or her relationship with the other parent.
- Show that you're pleased when your child reports enjoying the time spent with the other parent. Send your child off to the other home with a cheerful "Have a good time!"
- The best antidote to compartmentalization is cooperation. Offer a united front with your ex to help your child when he or she is in distress.

Error 4

Competing for Your Child's Affection

INSTEAD OF FOCUSING on the child's needs, some parents vie with each other for their youngster's affection and loyalty. This behavior is particularly characteristic of controllers, who view much of life in win-lose terms.

Parental competition may take the form of showering a child with new possessions. While making home visits, I have seen shelves, closets, bookcases, and entire rooms overflowing with games, books, toys, dolls, and stuffed animals—more items than ten children could use. I have known parents to indulge their child, especially during a custody battle, with lavish vacations. One father whisked his young son off for a "weekend" in Alaska. The exhausted boy remembered only that the hotel in Anchorage had a great swimming pool. Some parents relax rules regarding chores, homework, and bedtime. They're afraid to limit the hours the child spends watching television or the type of movie he or she is allowed to see. To an insecure parent, saying no carries the risk of incurring the child's anger. To win affection, the parent may do the child's homework, take him or her to pricey restaurants, or go to extraordinary means to provide "fun" activities. Such a father or mother has been called a Disneyland dad or Disneyland mom.

The competition can become intense, sometimes outlandish. I have seen parents vie in throwing the most expensive or creative birthday parties. If one parent takes a child to the beach, the other feels compelled to do the same. If the financial positions of the parents are unequal, the more affluent takes full advantage.

The child responds to this competition by exploiting both parents. The youngster utilizes emotional blackmail, capitalizing on any advantage he or she perceives. It's ugly to see a child try to hold one parent to the standard set by the other. Whatever concession he or she has been able to wrest from one parent will be held up to the other. If you look closely at what's really occurring, you'll see that this behavior has little to do with who loves whom, or whether the child is asking for a demonstration of commitment. The child is using both parents without respecting either.

A young child's willingness to stay overnight with a parent can become a battleground. Ginger's father accused her mother of instilling fear in their five-year-old daughter so that she refused to stay overnight with him in his new town house. By pushing for overnight visitation as hard as he could, this man alienated his daughter. At one point Ginger told me, "I don't even like seeing him." Ginger's father had only pushed because he thought he was losing ground in a competition with his spouse. He failed to realize that some young children feel extremely insecure after the family breaks up, that it takes time before they are ready to stay overnight in an unfamiliar place. It is a psychological or developmental issue that has nothing to do with whether the child loves the parent.

Ginger's dad, assuming that his spouse was trying to subvert his relationship with his daughter, was prepared to take the matter to court, hoping the judge would order his daughter to have overnights. In a report to the court, I stated: "Overnight visitation is not a trophy to be won or lost. At issue should be what will foster [Ginger's] trust in each parent and provide comfort. The best interest of the child does not involve forcing her to stay overnight at her father's home." I pointed out that as Ginger developed a more positive relationship with her father, she would look forward to visits, feel more at ease, and eventually desire to spend the night. A court battle was pointless and wasteful. The judge denied the petition for overnight visitation. Stating that the child needs "a normal life," he ordered both parents to consult with a psychologist monthly.

If one parent is engaged in a competitive struggle but the other is not, the child may not understand what's going on. He or she basks in the attention that the competitive parent is showering upon him, but has no idea what the true motive is. This puts the noncompetitive parent at a temporary disadvantage.

Roger was intent on a 50-50 custody arrangement. Penny wanted something more like a 75-25 division. Their twelve-year-old son, Richard, stated emphatically that he wanted to spend half the time with each parent. In writing, he laid out a detailed schedule showing exactly how the time should be divided from week to week. Richard was furious at his mother for not agreeing to what his father wanted. Never had I encountered a child of this age who was so wrapped up in the intricacies of a custody arrangement. As I came to know the family, it was apparent that the father had discussed the matter at great length with his son. He competed to gain the boy's sympathy by portraying himself as the victim of his wife, who against his wishes had instigated divorce proceedings. Playing on Richard's sense of fairness, he persuaded his son that 50-50 would be best.

Richard found his father convincing mainly because his was the only point of view the child heard. Richard's mother told him that custody was something for her and his dad to work out. Although tempted to defend herself and counter all that Richard had heard from her husband, Penny remained silent on the subject. Given that his dad talked to him so often about the custody feud, Richard grew frustrated by what seemed to him to be his mom's secrecy. In the short term, Penny paid a high price, because Richard became increasingly resentful and hostile, but I believe she did the right thing for her son by not entering into a competition.

Some parents who have had little involvement in their children's lives change dramatically after they separate. There are two reasons for this, one positive, the other definitely not. On the one hand, as a single parent a father or mother is virtually compelled to spend more time with a child than he or she did before. The parent now has to oversee some of the most routine aspects of a child's daily care as well as make important decisions. After separating, some mothers and fathers discover what they were missing and become better parents. They find that they enjoy involvement in many aspects of their child's life that they had had nothing to do with before.

On the other hand, some parents blossom suddenly into father or mother of the year as part of a carefully crafted strategy in the custody battle. This is not about the child. It is about competing and winning. After the final custody order is issued, these parents revert to spending little or no time with their child. Imagine how crushing it is for a child to revel in all a parent's newfound attention, believing he or she merits it, only to have that parent withdraw after the divorce settlement.

Wayne asserted that he had been the responsible, stable, nurturing parent of two sons. He claimed that his wife had been so busy gratifying her own needs that she had been only peripherally involved in the boys' lives. Christy responded that her husband was a vindictive person who would do anything to hurt her. This turned out to be the case. During the custody evaluation Wayne attacked almost every aspect of her personality and functioning as a mother. He warned how miserable her life would be once he obtained custody.

Christy stated that her husband had been an absentee father right up until the separation. On weekends, holidays, and whenever he took a day off from work, he was out on the golf course and enjoying other pursuits of interest solely to him, spending little time with their sons. When Christy had errands to run, she occasionally would ask her husband to watch the boys rather than drag them with her. Instead of welcoming the time alone with them, Wayne demanded that she hire a sitter even though he planned to remain in the house. She recalled that one night she asked her husband to purchase dessert for one of the boys' birthday parties. He left, visited a friend, and returned when the party was nearly over.

Both adults had deficiencies as parents. However, most of Wayne's assertions about his wife were twisted interpretations or exaggerations of actual events. When he criticized his wife for being short-tempered, he omitted mentioning what he did to provoke her. Collateral sources described Christy as the primary caretaker of the boys, involved day-to-day in their educational, recreational, and religious activities. Praise for her as a mother was consistent and uniform.

Christy acknowledged that since the separation her husband had changed for the better. He was more involved with their sons than ever and seemed to enjoy it. Christy was delighted that the boys were benefiting from the fatherly attention they had hungered for. She hoped her husband had truly changed his ways, but she feared that his involvement might only be part of his campaign to defeat her. Never did Christy regard custody as a competition. More than anything, she wanted a cooperative relationship.

Christy's mounting hope that her husband's involvement with their sons would last was shattered by a chilling statement he made as the custody evaluation was drawing to a close. Wayne warned her that if he failed to obtain sole custody, he would stop seeing the children. He proclaimed that within a few years they all would come crawling to him. Wayne was furious that I recommended joint legal custody with the children residing primarily with their mother. Unfortunately, he proceeded to carry out his threat. He stopped seeing his children for overnight visits and insisted that they be withdrawn from the school where they were thriving. Christy reported that her husband continued threatening to leave her in such poverty that she would have no choice but to relinquish the children to him.

Driven by their insecurities or their desire to control, parents intensify the competition to win over the child and defeat their spouse. As the parental relationship becomes more acrimonious, there can be no winner. There is only a loser—the child!

Correction: Cooperate—Don't Compete

In an intact marriage, mothers and fathers who think first and foremost of their children are partners, not rivals. During and after divorce proceedings, problem solvers still focus on how to co-parent. Unfortunately, some parents decide to cooperate only after they experience the high casualties of custody warfare. Drained by the expenditure of time, money, and energy, they come to realize that everyone is worse off than ever.

How do you cooperate with someone you can't stand to talk to, much less be around? Remember, you once saw enough good in your spouse to fall in love and marry. The good qualities haven't all vanished. Focus on those, and carefully consider what he or she can offer your child. Taking this approach will be a lot more conducive to cooperation than dwelling on the shortcomings.

One father exhibited remarkable determination to emphasize the positive in a situation that was devastating to his two sons. Suffering from an acute psychiatric illness, Dennis's wife, Cynthia, left home and moved in with her mother, who lived several hundred miles away. She alleged that Dennis had abused her and refused to return to the state where the marital home was located to spend time with her children. Dennis drove five hours so they could visit Cynthia regularly during their summer vacation. He allowed Cynthia unlimited access to the boys by telephone. When she came for interviews during the custody evaluation and still refused to stay overnight in the area so that she could have an extended visit with the boys, Dennis left work early so they could spend time with her before she departed for the airport. Despite his frustration with these circumstances and his anger over her allegations, this father accommodated his wife in order to help his children, who missed their mother very much. Through it all he maintained that before she became ill she had been a superb wife and mother.

In some situations, it's difficult to find positive qualities upon which to focus. A parent not only may want to avoid a spouse who has been neglectful or abusive but also may want to keep the child as far away from that person as possible. Trish had remarried and thought her life was on track. Out of the blue her ex-husband, Willis, called and asked to see their boy. Years had passed since Willis had deserted her and their very young child. Trish knew that she could fight Willis and end up in a major court battle, expecting that if the court hearing did not go Willis's way, he would persist, harassing her and disrupting her family's life.

Instead of following her gut instinct to try to shut Willis out of her life, she and her current husband met with him. They learned that Willis was living in the area, had a job, and was self-supporting. Their son had been asking questions about his father and wanted to see him, so Trish agreed to brief father-son visits. These went far better than she had anticipated, and the child began spending time with his father on a regular basis. It took a lot for this woman to bury the past and think about her son's needs and the overall welfare of her family.

When you have an important decision to make, it's not easy to consult a person whose opinion you no longer value. Still, it's usually worth the goodwill that's fostered when a parent shares information and at least seeks the other's opinion. In joint custody arrangements, information sharing and consultation are mandated by the court, but no court can mandate people's attitude toward each other. Even if you were to have sole custody of your child, the other parent is part of that youngster's life. The manner in which you choose to communicate can reduce the tension or add to it. Attempting to exclude or ignore the other parent just because you have primary custody harms your child. By demonstrating that you value what your spouse can offer, you help your child and make life easier for yourself.

You can cultivate a cooperative attitude toward your spouse or ex-spouse by:

- Thinking about the good qualities of the other parent.
- Sparing the criticism and focus on what the other parent can offer your youngster.
- Remembering you are not in competition with your ex-spouse; the issue is helping your child.
- Bearing in mind that a cooperative attitude may go a long way in deflecting hostility and make life easier for both you and your child.
- Maintaining appropriate discipline. Your child needs loving limits.
- Stop being a Disneyland dad or mom. Your lesson to your child should be that things don't matter, people do. Focus your time with your child on doing both everyday things (which provides a comforting sense of routine) and things that emphasize togetherness over expense (cooking a meal together; visiting a museum or library; going on a long walk, hike, or bike ride; doing a craft or building project).

Error 5

Aligning Other People Against Your Ex

With their world falling apart, divorcing parents naturally turn to family, friends, and work colleagues. Coping with depression, anxiety, and anger, they confide in these trusted individuals, ask their opinions, and enlist their support. But I've watched what began as a healthy search for emotional support turn into a pernicious campaign to marshal opinion favorable to a parent's custody case. A parent sees it as a notch in his or her belt each time a person is converted to this parent's point of view and becomes an ally. This parent lines that person up for use during litigation. The parent finds emotional gratification in turning formerly neutral individuals against the spouse, and winning over someone who had been primarily the spouse's friend or relative is an even bigger triumph.

People who are close to a couple find it hard to remain neutral as a divorce occurs. Relatives on one side may sever contact with the other side of the family. Although they prefer to avoid choosing sides, neighbors and friends find it hard not to. An unscrupulous controlling parent maneuvers neighbors and friends into having to choose. Conversing often and intimately, doing favors, and buddying up to their children, the parent insinuates himself or herself more into their lives. Although the recipients of all this attention may be puzzled, they're not likely to turn away the divorcing parent. Unknowingly, they're being drawn into the case the parent is mounting.

As reluctant as relatives, neighbors, and friends are to be embroiled in a custody battle, they will participate as witnesses if convinced that it's the right thing to do to help a child. As a custody evaluator, I ask each parent to provide a list of collateral sources, individuals who can relate direct personal observations (versus what they have heard) about the family. Particularly helpful are relatively unbiased sources such as teachers, counselors, pediatricians, psychotherapists, activity leaders (e.g., coaches, Scout masters), and clergy. I also find it informative to interview people who have known the family over time, such as relatives, neighbors, friends, and work supervisors and colleagues. Although family members usually support their own in custody battles, they have useful observations and sometimes helpful insights. In one case, a grandparent had spent many hours each month in the marital home visiting and babysitting. She revealed a lot about what went on that I had heard from no one else, including her own daughter, the mother of the children.

During custody evaluations, there's no confidentiality because everything is discoverable through the legal process. Usually the people with whom I speak are candid, sometimes quite emotional, because they are genuinely concerned about the child; they are flattered that they've been identified as important sources of information and think they can have an impact on what happens; or they have become intensely partisan and find excitement in joining the fray. Sometimes a person intensely dislikes one of the parents and seizes the opportunity to address his or her own issues, some not especially relevant to the child's situation. For example, a grandparent who has long disapproved of his in-law is eager to get a lot off his chest.

Asked for a list of collateral sources, Ronald and Beth responded so quickly that I suspected they'd been mulling this over for some time. Indeed, their entire neighborhood had become privy to the details of their marital turmoil, the street turned into a war zone in which longtime friends and neighbors found themselves polarized. So self-centered were Ronald and Beth that they didn't notice as the neighbors, suffering from battle fatigue, grew disgusted with both of them. One woman commented, "There were points where all of us as neighbors wanted to back out. They've played the neighborhood to an extreme. . . . It got to a point where we wouldn't go outside. We didn't want to get caught in a confrontation."

A father expressed a similar opinion: "It is a slash and burn mentality. It's trashed not only a marriage but a couple of kids and had an impact on the neighbors. It's the darndest thing I've ever seen, systematically tearing lives apart, and their children's lives, and several other relationships. . . . My wife and I have been severely manipulated." He noted bitterly that Ronald's and Beth's problems had infiltrated his own marriage. "This has caused problems for my wife and me. My wife sides with [Beth] and believes she's a victim. [Ronald] has tried to convince me his wife wasn't all there and he had to do what he had to do." This man's wife told me that, just as she was leaving to run an errand, Ronald would rush over to regale her husband with the latest horror story about Beth.

One neighbor said what I ultimately found to be true: "There was no stable environment. It is both their faults. They weren't concerned about the kids. It was all [Ronald and Beth]."

Remember that your child's neighborhood—with playmates

and their parents he or she knows well—is an ongoing support system. If you polarize that support system and turn people away from your ex, where will that leave your child? Will the neighbors be as willing to watch out for your family as before? Will play dates be forthcoming? At a time when your child craves stability, lining up allies can mean undermining that need. Your child can't afford that.

Psychotherapists who work with children during custody battles try to avoid being drawn into litigation. They don't want the therapeutic relationship to be compromised by having to turn over records or testify. More than one parent has terminated a child's psychotherapy because he or she anticipated that the therapist might discredit the parent's position in the custody lawsuit. Mel and Paula's son, Cecil, was "falling apart" under the emotional stress of his parents' warfare. The therapist's blunt advice to stop fighting in front of the child fell on deaf ears. During individual meetings with the therapist, each parent was building a case. Sadly, the therapist observed, "They had no interest in working together," even when their son began thinking about suicide.

Eventually Paula terminated the therapy. She was angry at the therapist for meeting separately with the father and upset by the therapist's disagreeing with her about what custody arrangement would be best for Cecil. The final straw was the therapist stating that she did not want to testify in the upcoming hearing because doing so would compromise her relationship with Cecil and violate his confidentiality. A year later, when I asked this same therapist to treat another child caught in the cross fire of a parental custody dispute, she told me that she no longer works with children under such circumstances.

I have known parents to take a child clandestinely to a therapist for months before the other parent found out. When there is not yet a formal custody order, a parent can get away with this more easily. (Under most custody arrangements, a parent is required to inform the other of medical and mental health treatment.) The therapist encounters a concerned parent and a needy child. The parent fills the therapist's ear with insidious comments, attributing the child's difficulties to the parent the therapist has never met. As the child continues in treatment, the therapist eventually will start wondering why he has heard nothing from the other parent. Upon contacting him or her, the therapist finds out that the other parent had no idea the child was being treated. A parent may discover that his or her youngster is in therapy quite by chance when the child casually alludes to regularly talking with an adult whom the parent has never heard of. In the meantime, the mother or father already bringing the child to therapy has been cultivating another ally.

If you're dedicating your efforts to winning your child's therapist over to your side, remember that the goal of therapy is ultimately to provide your child with a safe haven to discuss his or her fears and anxieties and receive emotional support in a time of crisis. If you present the therapist with biased information designed to undermine your ex and shore up support for your case, you're risking the therapist's ability to give your child the best help. It's easy to underestimate how confused and guilty children can feel at this time; they need all the help they can get.

A parent may try to convince a therapist or custody evaluator that a person close to the other spouse is a bad influence or a danger to the child. Jealousy or the desire to curry favor with the mental health professional may be the motive, but the parent would never see it that way. Tim's parents were deceased, but Liz's parents were still living. After he and Liz separated, Tim did all he could to convince me that his in-laws were a terrible influence on the children. He went so far as to allege that Liz's father had many years ago sexually abused a niece and fondled his granddaughter. The mother of the niece would not allow her daughter, now an adult, to discuss the matter with me. There was no evidence that the grandfather had behaved inappropriately toward his granddaughter. In fact, after the incident allegedly occurred, Tim permitted the children to visit the grandparents without his being present. I knew that the children loved their maternal grandparents and wanted to spend time with them. I had no proof that the grandfather posed a danger to anyone. I suspected Tim was jealous of the emotional and financial support her parents offered Liz, especially during the divorce proceedings. He was without family support, so he sought to convert me to his side.

What will the children think if Tim's shadowy allegations result in removing Grandpa from their lives? Will they imagine they have done something wrong? Will they wonder if Grandpa is mad at them or doesn't want to see them? As I write this, I continue to evaluate the situation and am leaning heavily toward recommending that the grandfather be allowed to spend time with his grandchildren unsupervised.

The child's school is supposed to be neutral territory. Nonetheless, disputatious parents may try to drag educators into the fray. Parents may cozy up to teachers by volunteering in classrooms, chatting with teachers before school, requesting extra conferences, and conversing on the telephone. During these contacts, they dish out the latest dirt on their spouses. Most teachers are not so susceptible to these shenanigans and are uncomfortable with a parent who attempts to air dirty laundry. But there may be subtle effects. If their contact is mainly with one parent, teachers may erroneously believe that the other is less interested in the child's education. This kind of lobbying can contaminate the teacher's relationship with the child.

Baby-sitters, nannies, and other child-care providers frequently get roped into custody disputes. Formerly, these people were employees of both parents. After the separation, unless both parents are paying their salaries, they work for just one or they are out of a job. Most child-care providers prefer to remain neutral if they worked for the whole family. Otherwise their loyalty is to the parent currently employing them. Many child-care providers are recent immigrants who find it frightening to be questioned in a language not their own by psychologists or lawyers, let alone to testify in a deposition or trial.

Before providing any information, Nina, who worked as a nanny, told me she didn't want to go to court. What she relayed to me was fairly typical of a person who is still being paid by both parents and seeks to offend neither. As soon as she made a positive statement about one parent, she felt compelled to do the same regarding the other. Just after she asserted that the father is "very friendly, very nice" and commented that the mother "is more quieter," Nina quickly added, "They're both nice." Although another provider of child care had described one of the children as moody, aggressive, and extremely unpredictable, Nina would have had me think this boy was an angel. It seemed evident that Nina was astute enough to realize that if she restricted herself to bland but positive statements, she could avoid antagonizing either employer and probably get out of testifying.

Other child-care providers find it difficult to remain neutral. They believe that their bread and butter depends upon supporting their employer's position. One mother managed to induce Maria, a nanny still working for her ex-husband, to talk to her. Clandestinely in her car, the mother grilled Maria about what went on in the father's home. The mother warned Maria that her ex-husband had had many nannies, that they didn't last long, and that some seemed to disappear. The mother induced the nanny to tell her enough so that she was certain she would be a compelling and essential witness. She totally miscalculated. Fiercely loyal to her employer, Maria provided him with a full report of her meeting with his ex-wife. The father had no reservations about allowing Maria to spend an hour with me. Maria decided to tell me anything I needed to know, hoping that she would be spared from having to go to court. Her impression of the mother was far from positive.

Naturally, I wondered whether Maria was telling each person what he or she wanted to hear. To the mother, she made statements about how the father was both neglectful and permissive. To the father, Maria described his ex-wife as though she were in immediate need of intensive psychiatric care. The point is that a conscientious young woman who cared about children was imposed upon by two parents who despised each other. Each hoped that Maria's statement would bolster the case he or she was building. Maria didn't stick around for long. She gave her employer notice and took another position. Baby-sitters or nannies are generally an affectionate, stable influence in your child's life. Why jeopardize this support in the hope of gaining a temporary ally?

Finally, in trying to influence and boost credibility with a third party, such as a custody evaluator (or even a judge), a parent may use his or her own child. The parent's thinking is that if the information comes directly from the youngster, it carries more weight. I have seen letters children supposedly wrote on their own to a judge explaining why they want to live with one parent. It didn't take a detective to determine that the children had adult assistance in composing these messages. Parents have told their children what to say to a therapist, again expecting the information will have greater credibility if it emanates from the child. I have received messages and calls that I found suspect because of the manner in which they were communicated. A youngster obtained my phone number from a parent, signifying that a parent was involved from the outset. Similarly, faxes, typed letters, and the like imply an adult's hand, as does certain wording. It is highly unusual for young children to call an adult they don't know very well, much less a person who has heretofore been a total stranger.

If the youngster had a good relationship with relatives, friends, and neighbors before the parents separated, he or she may now see them much less frequently or not at all. One boy told me, "I was thinking about the [Smiths]. Now my dad thinks they're on my mom's side. I don't think they're on anyone's side." Whatever was true, this boy rarely had contact with these lifelong friends, seeing them only occasionally when he was spending time with his mother. People the child has known most of his life behave differently around him. The child senses that some subjects, especially anything relating to the parent who is now persona non grata, are off limits.

Imagine how hard it is for a child to maintain a relationship with a person he or she knows you detest. Just having warm feelings about that individual might seem tantamount to treason. For example, your child would know it was no longer acceptable to love an adoring aunt because you've vilified her. While fighting for custody, you may gain new allies, but your child stands to lose precious human contacts.

Correction: Support Your Child's Positive Relationships with Relatives, Neighbors, Professionals, and Friends

Your anger toward your spouse can spread like a fire, threatening to destroy relationships important to your child. As the family splits up, try to preserve the relationships your child has. Remember, your youngster receives comfort and security by maintaining ties to relatives, neighbors, professionals, and friends who have cared about him or her. The fact that you can't stand your spouse is no reason for your child to endure more losses. Rather than destroy a relationship that's important to your child, bite your tongue and do what it takes to remain on civil terms, even with a person who is sympathetic to "the other side." This requires restraint and a long-term perspective.

In-law conflicts, often the butt of jokes, exist even in some of the strongest marriages. When a divorce occurs, old grievances, like cancers in remission, return, more malignant than ever. In-laws who have always disapproved of their offspring's selection of a spouse feel vindicated. The son- or daughter-in-law feels equally vindicated in earlier opinions about the in-laws. Divorcing, some parents are primed to do what they could only fantasize in the past—minimize or sever contact between their child and the grandparents. But in so doing, they can destroy a powerfully stabilizing influence for their child.

Of course, there are some situations in which it is best that a grandparent have little or no contact with the grandchildren; for example, when a grandparent interferes with or undermines the parents or has psychological problems of his or her own that would adversely affect the child. But these circumstances are different from excluding involved, adoring grandparents because of a vendetta.

What is called for is for you to overcome your desire to retaliate for something that happened in the past. The mother of your son's best friend may be on your enemy list because she said unkind things about you to the custody evaluator. What are you going to do—tell your child he can't play with his buddy? Overlooking the insult and being civil to the other parent will allow your son to continue enjoying his friend.

Harold learned that his wife had worked on their son's teacher so that the teacher had formed a poor opinion of him as a parent. Thanks to Abigail's unabashed campaign to curry favor not only with the classroom teacher but also with the school counselor, both of these professionals developed the impression that, although Harold was well-intentioned, he was incompetent as a parent. Harold, in fact, was a caring, involved father. He attended parent-teacher conferences and was interested in all aspects of his son's life. Unlike his wife, however, he hadn't been dropping by constantly. After conferring with school personnel, I questioned Harold and informed him that the school didn't have a very positive view of him compared with the glowing opinion of his wife.

A parent in Harold's position might well have felt humiliated, then furious, not just at his wife but at the teacher and counselor for being sucked in and appearing to take sides. He might have concluded that the school was hopelessly partisan. He might even have decided that this was the wrong facility to educate his child and sought to enroll him elsewhere.

Fortunately, Harold was not thin-skinned or inclined to react precipitously. He took in stride Abigail's campaign to vilify him. He understood why school personnel might form opinions based on their heavy exposure to her. Harold knew that withdrawing his son from that school would hurt him, and his wife would go on to poison people at the next school. Instead, he asked himself how he could remedy the current problem. He decided to spend more time at the school to convince the teacher and counselor that he wanted to be the best parent he could. This would also require following their advice about how he could help his son, who was struggling academically and socially.

Despite your feelings, you may have to go out of your way to help your child preserve relationships. Your youngster may need guidance on how to reply when other youngsters or adults ask about the family situation. If the child has a close relationship with a relative who lives far away, you are responsible for taking the extra steps to be sure that distance doesn't become a convenient pretext for the relationship to languish or end.

It's easy to let what you feel toward the other parent color everything related to that person. Relationships beneficial to a child can be destroyed when a parent indiscriminately perceives everyone on "the other side" as evil and voices how he or she feels. Lena provides a superb example of how a parent can swallow resentment, thereby helping her child preserve an important relationship.

Lena and her husband were in the midst of a bitter divorce. She knew that some members of his family had said very mean things about her. Lena struggled against her automatic inclination to tar all of her husband's relatives with the same brush. Her daughter Betsy had a school assignment to write about a person she admired. Lena told me of her chagrin when Betsy composed an essay about her paternal grandmother. The child's paternal grandparents and Lena had always had a strained relationship. Although Lena was critical of her in-laws when speaking of them to me, she did not utter one negative word about them to her daughter. Since separating from her husband, Lena had cooperated with him so that Betsy could spend time with the grandparents even though they lived hundreds of miles away. Lena never interfered with correspondence or phone calls between Betsy and the grandparents. Betsy thrived under the extended family support.

To support your child's cherished relationships and relationships with professionals:

- Don't allow your dislike of a person to destroy your child's relationship with that individual.
- Do whatever it takes to help your child retain contact with people who have been important in his or her life; bite your tongue and remain civil.
- Actively encourage friends, relatives, and professionals to remain a part of your child's life. Acknowledge the awkwardness but make it clear that your priority is your child's stability.
- Help maintain your youngster's relationship with grandparents who may be very important to him.
- Remember that good baby-sitters are hard to find. Don't risk your child's relationship with a beloved nanny by making demands or influencing her to take sides.
- Don't secretly try to co-opt neutral parties, such as teachers or therapists, who are endeavoring to help your child.

Error 6

Exposing Your Child to Adult Issues

Protecting your child requires that you not embroil him in adult issues that are upsetting and beyond his control. Insulate him from wrangling over finances, custody conflicts, and details of legal proceedings.

Many parents fail to exercise self-restraint or, worse still, involve their child in the war. Children have told me that a parent coached them on what to say during a custody evaluation. These youngsters were grilled after each interview and prepared for the next. Some trusted me enough to confide their resentment at parental meddling. A nine-year-old boy reported that his dad called him early in the morning at his mother's to say, "I heard you're going to Dr. Samenow. You better tell the truth." In this case the truth was what the boy's dad deemed it should be. Fearful that his father might find out what he said to me, the youngster anticipated, "He'll get mad and will end up spanking me."

Some children get bombarded by a parent's constant discussion of divorce and custody. One child of divorce, now an adult, is still appalled that her mother shared stories of sexual dissatisfaction with her then-teenage daughter. Others are upset by what they overhear.

Ten-year-old Bradley was distraught when, from another room, he heard his dad's conversation with a friend. Both men were boasting loudly about "winning custody," the friend about already having "won" it in his own case and Bradley's dad proclaiming he would "win" it in his. Bradley cringed at the names his dad called his mom, then was furious when he heard the other man agree she was a bitch.

I have been dismayed by the lack of restraint on the part of some parents who ventilate their anger to their offspring with no holds barred. Discouraged over the course of the custody battle with his wife, a father poured out his frustration to his two children, telling them he might have to abandon them by moving abroad, where he still had supportive relatives. On another occasion, he said that the children's mother was draining him financially to a point that he might have to move into a nearby house that had only two rooms. Worried that there would be no space for her and her brother, the little girl said sadly that her daddy would never be able to see them again.

I was so appalled by this man's outbursts that I confronted him directly. Defensive but calm, he replied, "I believe in telling the kids the truth. I fear I won't win a battle of innuendos and half-truths. If half-truths and innuendos prevail, as they have, I'll lose and be a second cousin once removed to my kids. . . . If I have to 'get a life' as the saying goes, and the kids are on the way to being grown, that's an option that's a possibility for me." These words were uttered by the very same father who had earlier told me about being the devoted parent "who held the children's hands and comforted them through stitches and emergency rooms." Ultimately I recommended that the children reside primarily with their mother and spend alternate weekends, alternate holidays, and a major part of the summer with the father with whom they had, for the most part, a positive relationship. Even after my recommendations were adopted and the litigation concluded, the children continued to hear their father's expressions of disgruntlement with his career, his worsening financial plight, and his perpetual complaints about his ex-wife.

In another situation, a child found himself up for grabs as his parents went to war. He was delivered to my office for an interview by his father, who left to run a brief errand. Minutes later the door to the waiting room opened and in came the child's mother, who immediately spirited him away beyond the immediate jurisdiction of the court. The boy was traumatized by the abduction, even though it was by his mother. She took him to an unfamiliar home in a strange neighborhood, and his daily routine was disrupted as he was kept in hiding. Later the mother brought him back and the custody process went forward in the court.

With adult nerves frayed and tempers short, children may suddenly find themselves in the midst of a serious altercation. With her new husband, a mother was watching her son play in a high school basketball game. As they were leaving, the boy's father, who had watched the game from another area of the gym, passed the stepfather, and sharp words were exchanged. The father loudly claimed the stepfather had shoved him and threatened to file assault charges. Although no one was physically hurt, the father seized upon the exchange as an opportunity to harass his ex-wife and her husband, all in front of the children, who were very upset.

Damage can be done whether something untoward happens spontaneously or someone acts in a calculating and vicious manner. Upon being presented with his wife's bill of complaint and a restraining order, a father was compelled to leave the marital home. He was so outraged that he decided to show the legal papers to his twelve-year-old daughter, seeking her sympathy and support. A bill of complaint spells out the grounds that a spouse cites in seeking a divorce. In this instance, the document mentioned a number of sensitive matters. Quite appropriately the parents had never told the child about any of them, including a suicide attempt by the father.

After the father gave the document to his daughter to read, he told her that it was exaggerated and inaccurate. She went to her mother, demanding to know why her dad was being forced to leave their home. Her mother responded with an appropriately vague explanation. Continuing to use his daughter as a confidante, the father inflamed her to the point that a wedge was driven between her and her mother. The mother was paying a huge price by keeping her mouth shut about adult matters that should never have been broached by either parent. But she did the right thing.

Mothers and fathers have dragged their children to court hearings when their presence was not required. In fact, there was no reason for them even to know that a hearing was occurring. Being at a courthouse meant that the child was missing school or an activity. Because children cannot accompany their parents into the courtroom during divorce or custody proceedings, they must wait alone or with a sitter. Some parents want to put their children on the stand. But they are thinking only of themselves if they even suggest this to their offspring. I cannot think of a time when a judge permitted a child to testify in open court for one parent and against another during a custody proceeding. The potential trauma for such a child is enormous.

Occasionally, a judge asks to interview a youngster privately in chambers. But even when a child indicates a willingness to speak to a judge privately, there is potential for emotional damage. With adolescent bravado, a boy asserted to me that he was eager to tell a judge whom he wanted to live with. The custody hearing was nasty, and the judge decided to talk with the boy. Leaving the courthouse, I encountered the child and his mother about to enter the building. All the boy's nerve and bluster had vanished. He said he had had nightmares about coming to court and still worried that he might have to testify in front of his parents and their lawyers. He admitted that he had considered running away the previous day. I reassured him that the judge was a kind woman and would talk to him alone. He looked relieved and said that as long as it was in private that was fine. He loved both his parents and didn't want to hurt either. I don't know what the teenager told her behind closed doors, but the judge accepted my recommendation that the father retain sole custody.

Parents all too often discuss financial matters with their children. True, youngsters cannot be completely insulated from such conversations. It is a reality that the funds available determine what a youngster can do from day to day and general lifestyle, everything from the food on the table to whether he or she can purchase sports equipment or play video games. However, there are ways to discuss money that are helpful and appropriate to the maturity of the child.

Unfortunately, with a divorce looming, boys and girls may be exposed to mean-spirited contests over money. Twelve-year-old Janet's haven was her school, which happened to be private and expensive. There was a possibility that her parents might not be able to pay for it in the future. However, they didn't have to draw her into the details of their financial situation. Throughout the academic year following her parents' separation, she worried about whether she would have to go elsewhere the next year. I could see Janet wince when, in my waiting room, she heard her father announce that he would pay for her school even if it required taking two jobs. Janet loved her dad and felt guilty about burdening him. Even more confusing, her mother had been telling her that her dad earned enough to continue to afford the private school.

Nine-year-old Sam indicated that when his parents were together he knew little about their financial situation. Once they separated, he was hearing far more than he wanted. Previously discreet, Sam's mother began voicing her opinion about his dad's financial failure and irresponsibility. Sam told me, "I found out from my mom he wasn't doing too well at his business. I asked him just this week. He started telling me the truth about what was happening. He said . . . he had to fire an employee because he couldn't pay for her."

Sam grew concerned about his father's business, a worry he should not have had. As he was told more, he became confused because each parent was saying something completely different. Sam's mother could not have been thinking about him as she unleashed her vendetta against her husband. The father was drawn in because he was responding to his son's apprehension.

There are innumerable other controversies in which parents needlessly involve their offspring. By criticizing a spouse's business or career, a parent is likely to burden a child needlessly. The same is true with regard to the other parent's relationships with relatives, neighbors, friends, or business associates. Rarely is there reason to impart the details of the final divorce decree to a child.

Correction: Communicate Appropriately with Your Child (and Be Discreet with Your Ex)

Make a concerted effort to avoid drawing your child into the custody battle. Within hearing range, filter out of your discussions matters over which he or she has no control. Your child shouldn't be your confidant. Take pains not to unload your problems onto your son or daughter, who is powerless to do anything about them. Don't look to your child to fulfill needs that you are having trouble meeting yourself. Your child already has enough to contend with.

Of course, youngsters eventually become aware of financial issues if their standard of living changes—a smaller house, fewer trips to the shopping mall, less expensive birthday and Christmas gifts. When you talk about these changes, with as little emotion as possible stick to facts, and gear what you say to your child's level of understanding. You can calmly acknowledge the changes, then emphasize that you and your ex have worked out the current situation together. Say something like, "Yes, things are different, but we have plenty of money for the things we need and some for the things we want. Your father/mother and I don't want you worrying about money. We're fine. This is for the adults to handle."

If you and your spouse are feuding over money, don't assume that your child is equally caught up in financial matters. I have noticed that, unlike their parents, some children adjust quite well to having less in the way of material comforts or luxuries. This is an opportunity to put the emphasis on what really matters, not on possessions.

Stephanie and her two young sons left the marital residence and moved into a small furnished rental apartment. What Stephanie thought would be temporary quarters turned out to be their home for nearly three years. It was a drastic change for the boys from spacious separate rooms to sleeping in bunk beds in one small bedroom, no large playroom in the basement or family room in which to lounge and watch television. Even more serious, they lost their familiar community and the proximity of their old friends.

Stephanie was determined to make this situation comfortable while she worked and saved so that she could purchase a house. Rather than complain to the children, she emphasized what they could be grateful for. The complex had superb recreational facilities, including a pool, which the boys loved. There were other children to play with. Using decorative touches, Stephanie set about converting the sterile, cramped apartment into an inviting home. Although the boys visited their father in far more spacious quarters, they never made invidious comparisons. Perhaps the greatest plus was that Stephanie discovered they were living in one of the best school districts in the area, so when she was ready to buy a house, she chose to stay there.

Six-year-old Todd's father had been in prison, then in residential drug treatment. Janice and he had divorced and she had remarried, but their stormy and physically abusive relationship continued even after their separation. Janice had been relieved when her former husband was incarcerated because she didn't have to deal with him. Still, when her son asked about his dad, Janice gently let him know that he had been sick for a long time in a hospital.

Once Todd's father was released from residential drug treatment and was living in the community, he was eager to see his son. Skeptical that he had changed, Janice nonetheless cooperated with a therapist's suggestions for allowing Todd to have supervised visits with his father. She understood that telling Todd his father had been in jail would have served no useful purpose. In fact, it would have been deeply upsetting, for Todd had been holding on to fond memories of his dad. Intuitively, Janice grasped the point that there was always time in the future to disclose the full story, but her child needed to be protected until he could assimilate the information.

It's a challenge for a parent to keep his mouth shut when the other parent brings a new romantic partner into the child's life. But it does no good to run this person down to your child, even if you fear the newcomer is trying to replace you.

Sonya was smart enough to discover early the wisdom of keeping her fears to herself and her mouth shut. Sonya and Luke had separated but were not divorced. Temporarily, Luke was living at his "friend" Emma's home while looking for a house in the children's school district. Emma was discreet enough to leave at night when the children slept over, but Sonya remained upset that Emma was present almost all the rest of the time the children were with their father. The children told her that Emma made great pancakes and cooked everything from scratch. Sonya heard all about the cookies the kids baked with Emma. To her it was always "Emma does this" and "Emma does that." What really galled Sonya was that her daughter was drawn to Emma even more after Emma purchased two horses and kept them on the property.

Rather than complain and possibly lead the children to feel guilty over their relationship with Emma, whom they liked, Sonya took a different tack. Like it or not, Emma was in the picture, and Sonya could appreciate that the children enjoyed visits with their father, who was far more involved with them than before she and Luke separated. Sonya was secure enough to realize that Emma was no threat to her. If the children were enjoying Emma's cooking and her horses and liked Emma as a person, what could be wrong with that? It beat the alternative of their having to be around a woman whom they disliked or who disliked them.

You have had major differences with your ex-spouse, or you would still be married. And you will continue to have differences with your ex. But your child doesn't have to be witness to the conflicts. Children don't have to hear spats about which possessions should be kept at each home. They don't need to hear reprimands for late child support payments. There is no reason for them to be subjected to incessant bickering over one parent's alleged incursion into the other's time.

Protecting your child doesn't mean insulating him or her in a cocoon or denying that problems exist. Reasonable protection during separation and the aftermath of divorce entails the following:

- Don't discuss matters that don't concern your child, matters he or she is powerless to change anyway.
- Don't burden your child with information he or she isn't mature enough to assimilate.
- Don't use your child as a substitute spouse and have him or her shoulder adult burdens.
- Don't use your child as your confidant or therapist and thereby create a reversal of roles in which you expect him or her to support and advise you.

Error 7

Prematurely Introducing Your Child

to a New Love Interest

EVENTUALLY, MOST DIVORCING parents want to date. Feeling liberated from their spouses, some waste little time hiring sitters so they are free to go out. No matter when it occurs, if a parent enters into a relationship and involves the child, the youngster is suddenly competing with a stranger for the attention of his or her parent. What message does a child get when a parent fights for time with him or her, then opts to spend a significant amount of that time with someone else? What is a child to think when he or she perceives that one parent is trying to replace the other with a total stranger? In pursuit of companionship or sex, adults can be incredibly oblivious to the impact of their actions on their children.

Some divorcing parents introduce their newfound romantic partner on the pretext that he or she has children and they all should meet. They mistakenly think this perspective legitimizes the relationship. The result is the child having to share the parent not with one but with any number of strangers.

Take the case of a parent who develops a new relationship that seems to be going smoothly. The parent decides to introduce her child to this individual. The child likes the person, and an attachment develops. But when the relationship breaks up, the child suffers yet another loss. She has already lost the original family unit and the access she wants to both her parents. Now she is losing still another person she was beginning to care about.

In some instances, the parent's partner moves into the home. Like it or not, the child must now deal with this person as an ongoing presence. These situations usually turn out badly. The child resents the new person as an interloper. The romantic partner may not be fond of the child and may barely tolerate him or her or, worse, may be emotionally, physically, or sexually abusive. If the child complains to the parent, he or she may be ignored, disbelieved, or punished.

A psychologist evaluated ten-year-old Jerry and found him to be a casualty of a self-absorbed mother's insecurity and loneliness. Shortly after her marriage broke up, she invited a man to live in the house. After that relationship fell apart, she did the same with another. The psychologist wrote in his report: "[Jerry] sees that his mother is somewhat preoccupied with her own issues, which causes him a great deal of stress as he does not perceive that he is given all the attention that he needs at this critical stage when he is having problems. He views male figures within the home as unreliable, which again causes him a great deal of anxiety at this stage of his development." During psychological testing, Jerry made up a story in which the mother had "a new boyfriend who she is introducing to the children, but makes the children feel very sad." The psychologist noted that this boy "reports frequently feeling upset and that life is unfair."

Ariel's father and mother were divorced, and Ariel became attached to her dad's girlfriend, Cindy. With her mother working long hours, Ariel felt that she received more attention from and had more fun with Cindy. Ariel also developed a close relationship with Cindy's parents, spending days and occasional weekends with them. Referring to them as "my grandparents," Ariel explained, "I consider them real relations."

Ariel's father and Cindy had a tumultuous relationship. They had knock-down drag-out fights over the same issues with no resolution, but they were discreet enough to hide most of their discord from Ariel. Even after they broke up, the two of them would temporarily set aside their differences to spend weekends together with Ariel, who continued to speak fondly of eating "a family dinner." During the week, Ariel regularly chatted on the phone with Cindy. When her father chaperoned a Scout group on a field trip, he invited Cindy, which pleased Ariel.

Asked to draw a picture of her family, Ariel first drew Cindy. Asked about her three wishes, Ariel had no hesitation: "I have one good wish—that [Cindy] and Dad would get back together, and everyone would live happily ever after." Her next wish was that she would have no more baby-sitters, so that she could spend more time with her mother.

In this situation the father was neither thoughtless nor promiscuous. He and Cindy wanted a long-term relationship, but it didn't last in that form. Cindy was able to give Ariel time and attention, both of which were in short supply from her mother. Despite the precautions and the best of intentions on the part of both Cindy and Ariel's dad, Ariel experienced another devastating loss. Cindy told me, "[Ariel] has suffered a lot of loss. She doesn't believe Daddy and I have really separated. . . . [Ariel's] a really hurt little kid. I don't ever want her to feel I'm abandoning her."

It would have been far better had Ariel's father been with his girlfriend when Ariel was with her mother, spent time alone with his daughter, and not drawn his daughter into the maelstrom of his chaotic and volatile relationship with Cindy, only to have her life turned upside down when that relationship collapsed.

Correction: Introduce a New Romantic Partner Cautiously

Many divorced parents say that they need time to heal and have no interest in dating, declaring that the last thing they want in their lives is another man or woman. Others, feeling lonely and anxious, urgently seek out new relationships. Among this group are men and women, mostly women, who have never lived alone. Having moved from one situation of dependency to another, they've failed to acquire the self-confidence that develops through living on one's own. Still others feel incomplete, as though something is wrong with them unless they are involved in a relationship.

Going through a divorce, you have a lot to juggle without the entanglements and complications of a new relationship. I have stressed throughout this book that during this difficult time you must constantly make choices about priorities. Don't date at the expense of your child, who now, perhaps more than ever, requires lots of your time and undivided attention.

Almost as soon as the ink was dry on the divorce papers, Vincent became involved with a divorcée who also had a child. Moving in with her resulted in a major dilemma when it came to spending time with his eight-year-old daughter, Laura. Vincent's ex-wife, Nancy, adamantly refused to allow Laura to visit her father if the girlfriend was present. Nancy said she wanted Vincent and Laura to have a good relationship. However, Vincent had to determine what was more important, spending time with his daughter or spending time with his girlfriend. He couldn't do both simultaneously. Nancy suggested that Vincent rent an apartment so that he and Laura would have a home for just the two of them.

Although he loved his daughter, Vincent was caught up in his new romantic relationship and accused his ex-wife of being rigid, unreasonable, and jealous. He wanted her to accept reality; he was in love, he lived with this woman, and he saw no reason to conceal what was going on. Vincent contended that Laura would like his girlfriend and enjoy playing with her daughter. He thought it absurd to pay for a separate residence where he would spend little time, when Laura would have privacy and her own bedroom at his girl-friend's.

Nancy was ready to go to court to seek a protective order so that Laura wouldn't be exposed to the girlfriend. Vincent was in a bind. He couldn't meet the demands of his girlfriend and adhere to the visitation schedule that he had agreed to; sometimes he called Laura at the last minute, offering excuses for why he couldn't see her. According to Nancy, Laura became very upset when her father canceled visits.

I discussed this situation with Vincent, asking him to consider Laura's needs carefully. I said that his sharing another woman's bed was likely to be disturbing to Laura, and he needed to consider what kind of example he wanted to set. I also pointed out that he should be happy his daughter wanted to be with him.

I recommended to the attorneys and the court that Vincent not have Laura overnight when he was with his girlfriend. Because he regretted lying to his daughter and missing visits, Vincent decided to rent an apartment after all. He took my advice to discuss the situation with his girlfriend. I suggested that, if she weren't sympathetic, he consider whether he wanted to remain involved with a woman who pressured him to choose between her and his daughter.

I've seen children become hostile before they even met a parent's new boyfriend or girlfriend. Regardless of how solicitous that person is, the youngster sees only competition for his or her parent's attention and love or an attempted replacement for the other parent.

Shortly after Rita left her husband, she became involved with Sean and was eager for her sons to meet him. Sean did everything he could to hit it off with Max and Kevin. While acknowledging that Sean was nice to them, played games, and took them places, Kevin and Max remained indifferent. They voiced no specific objection to Sean, for there was hardly anything bad to say, but each boy complained to me that he never had time alone with his mother. Sean was always around! By spending little time alone with her children, Rita unintentionally was relegating Max and Kevin to second place, and the boys sensed it.

It's best not to date at all until you and your child are settled and have an established routine. Initially, limit your dating to times when your youngster isn't scheduled to be with you. Bringing new people in and out of your child's life is disruptive and breeds resentment.

If a relationship develops over many months (at least a half year), expose your child to your new partner gradually. When you do introduce your boyfriend or girlfriend, it should be through participation in activities outside the home, such as a sports event, a movie, or a day's outing. No matter how smoothly things seem to go, be sure you are continuing to spend time alone with your child. Don't rush to involve your boyfriend's or girlfriend's children, relatives, or friends with your child. Remember that, to your child, the more people there are to deal with, the less of you he or she has.

If you've known your partner for at least a year and are committed to a long-term relationship, have that individual spend increasing amounts of time with you and your child. See how well you all do together, then let the two spend time without you. Work out problems as they emerge, rather than ignore them or assume that they will disappear once you marry. Consider seeing a therapist jointly or sending your child separately to be sure your child feels free to discuss any problems.

Although you may have no desire to remarry, you may develop a stable romantic relationship. Whatever the character of the relationship, spend lots of time alone with your child. Introduce your partner gradually. If your son or daughter is getting along with that individual, doing things together will be a pleasure, not an imposition. I have known such relationships to enrich youngsters' lives.

After separating from her husband, Delores had more frequent contact with Raymond, a single neighbor. Gradually, a romantic relationship evolved in which the two spent a lot of time together. Delores's nine-year-old son, Trevor, already knew who Raymond was, since he lived nearby. Occasionally, Raymond stopped in to chat and sometimes stayed for a meal. Raymond talked to Trevor about school, soccer, and other subjects. Trevor warmed to the attention, and the two became good buddies. Eventually, Trevor began to confide in Raymond his unhappiness about his parents' divorce. All this developed gradually and naturally over time, without anyone trying to force anything. At no time did Raymond stay overnight. When he started taking trips with Delores and Trevor, he always slept in a separate room. Raymond was careful not to compete with Trevor's father and never saw himself as a substitute father.

If you find yourself in circumstances similar to these, use good judgment. No partner is a substitute parent unless the actual parent is literally unavailable to your child. You and your partner should not cohabit. You are not a family unit; don't try to pretend otherwise. Your child knows the difference. If you go away together and take your child, don't share a room with your partner (unless you are camping or are in a dormitory).

Whether or not you are thinking of marriage, be discreet in your romantic life. You have plenty of time for romance when the child is with the other parent. Physical displays of affection are likely to be upsetting until your child has become quite accustomed to the relationship. Even if you do plan to marry, I strongly caution you against living together before that occurs. If the relationship breaks up and your child has become attached, he or she will suffer another loss.

It is difficult to think constantly about the impact of what you're doing on your child. As you start to date and develop a relationship, be sensitive to your child's insecurity. He or she has lost a family and doesn't want to lose you.

You can use discretion and protect your child by doing the following:

- Don't try to force your child to like a person just because you do. Just as it took you time to decide whether you liked the individual in question, it will take your child time as well.
- Don't jeopardize your relationship with your child by subjecting him or her to the vicissitudes of your intimate relationships.
- Through what you say and do, assure your child that the person you are dating or marrying is not a replacement for his or her other parent.
- Be sure that your child has ample time with you and doesn't constantly have to share you with others.

V

Preserving Continuity

A FAMILY BREAKUP is traumatic for everyone. You and your spouse have many decisions and adjustments to make as you each build a new life. At the same time, your child needs to be protected and helped so that he or she can go on with life as smoothly as circumstances allow. It's up to you and your spouse whether during your divorce your child adjusts or becomes an emotional casualty of the strife between you.

Children move, change schools, and make friends under many circumstances. Not only do they survive but some develop greater self-confidence as they discover they can adapt. But most children do not welcome such changes when their parents are ending their marriage. Helpless to prevent their parents' divorce, they hang on to everything familiar and dear. They look for anything in their lives over which they might have some control.

By carefully thinking things through, you can do a lot to preserve continuity in your youngster's existence. Many children develop an emotional tie to the family home, so it helps for one parent to remain there if it's affordable. Otherwise, there are emotional and

221

logistical benefits to your child if you and your spouse reside near each other. It will help your child maintain stability if he or she can attend the same school and be near some close friends, and you can avoid unnecessary stress and save time for the important things if you're not driving him or her around to places that could be a walk or a bicycle ride away.

If it's necessary to find a new home, I recommend involving your youngster in the process, depending on her age and interest. Children have told me with excitement about their mom or dad taking them to look at houses, condos, or apartments. They're usually eager to give opinions and pleased to be involved in such an important matter, down to the details of deciding what color to paint their room, shopping for furniture, and arranging their belongings. Even if a child isn't interested in interior decor, he may well appreciate having some control over his life and will at the very least be glad to know his opinion still matters.

Be sure your child does not become a "latchkey kid," returning from school to a home where he spends hours each day with no adult supervision. Avoid plunking your child down at day care without thoroughly investigating the caregiver or the conditions. Take time to investigate and determine that he'll be spending time in safe, hygienic circumstances, cared for by a person who is responsible and knowledgeable enough about children to plan stimulating and enriching activities. Television is not a baby-sitter.

Rather than just react to events as they unfold, think about your priorities. In a busy life there's a great deal to juggle and many choices to be made. For the sake of continuity in your child's life, you may have to deny or postpone what you want for yourself. In a two-parent family, sacrifices are necessary. This is far more the case when only one parent is at home. Before making any new commitment, consider how much less time as a single parent you will have with your child. Do you really need to join the community association now? Work more hours to lobby for that promotion? Start that new business this year? Make time with your child your top priority. You'll never regret it.

I have stressed the importance of helping your child maintain close relationships with grandparents, other relatives, neighbors, and friends. Keeping things as they have been, even in small ways, can be comforting to your child. If it's at all feasible, help your child continue his Scout, religious, athletic, or other extracurricular activities with the friends who've been part of his or her life for some time. Keep the same doctor and dentist. Help maintain interests and hobbies.

If you must introduce a certain number of changes simultaneously into your child's life, establish a regular daily routine as quickly as you can. Having as much predictability as possible helps immeasurably.

Your attitude toward change is also critically important. Are your fears so intense that you maintain a pessimistic attitude toward life? Do you look at each adjustment you have to make as a burden or as an opportunity? Whatever the magnitude of the changes you are facing, you need to do two things: Help your child grieve and cope with his or her loss and guide him or her in perceiving the advantages of fresh starts. If you find yourself overwhelmed by the practical and psychological problems of divorce, do not hesitate to seek support from friends and assistance from a competent professional. If your child needs someone to talk to, find help for him or her.

★   ★   ★

Throughout this book I have emphasized the importance of approaching divorce and its aftermath as a problem solver rather than as a controller (or an impaired parent). I provided information about the legal system and examples of common—and avoidable—mistakes, advising you of the many problems that are likely to confront the entire family if you and your spouse become immersed in a custody battle rather than resolve your differences amicably. With information and sensitivity, you can make good choices. If you succeed in setting aside personal vendettas and approach separation and divorce as a problem to solve, you in fact will be acting in the best interest of your child.

Index

abduction of children, 119
abuse/assault, 18, 65, 67, 120, 137;
allegations of, 53, 55, 56, 116–22,
147–48; and deadly errors, 147–48,
154, 176, 186, 187, 194; and discovery,
91–92; and personality, 36–37, 40, 44,
53, 55, 56, 57, 91
alcohol, 98–99, 128, 149–50
aligning people against ex, 53, 189–201
American Academy of Matrimonial
Lawyers, 85
anger, 142–57, 181, 198, 203
attorneys: clients' relations with, 79–82;
and costs of custody warfare, 106–7,
109, 111–12, 121–22, 140; and court,
133, 134; and deadly errors, 140, 156,
160, 161; and discovery, 89–90, 104;
and mediation/negotiation, 80–82,
84–86; overview about, 76–82; and
personality, 38, 60, 79; selecting,
76–78; and self-representation, 136

baby-sitters/nannies. *See* child-care
providers
Brewer, Sanford L., 116

child custody: and child's needs, 64–65,
67, 68, 75; costs of warfare in, 1, 64,
105–22; court role in, 64–65, 132–38;
discovery in, 88–104; factors judges
consider in, 64–65; legal representation
during, 76–82; and mediation/
negotiation, 83–104; motives in, 1, 64;
and new relationships, 15; overview
about, 63–65; and preferences of child,
65; preparation for battles about,
87–104; revisiting agreements about,
75; types of, 64, 66–75. *See also*
custody evaluations; *type of custody*

child rearing, 9, 44–46
child-care providers, 25–26, 195–96, 201,
222
child/children: adulthood of, 16*n*, 27–28;
blame on, 114; as caretaker of parents,
49, 211; and choosing one parent over
another, 21–22, 72, 115, 139–40, 146,
156, 177; compartmentalization of life
of, 169–79; competing for affection of,
180–88; daily life of, 24–25, 164–65,
221–23; dumping on, 164, 177, 208;
empathy for, 163–68; exploitation of
parents by, 181; exposure to adult
issues of, 202–11; feelings of lack of
control by, 19–20, 21, 222; guilt of,
23, 139, 143, 175, 193, 207, 210;
hiding misery by, 2–3; interests of, 133,
136, 140, 150, 155, 186; judges'
interviews of, 123, 205–6; lives apart
from both parents, 49–51; as in middle,
41, 49–50, 139–40, 146; needs of,
64–65, 67, 68, 75, 163–68; as
pawns/mouthpieces, 88, 115–16,
120–21, 130, 161, 182–83, 196–97,
202; preferences of, 65, 129, 171–72;
psychological scars of, 2, 16*n*, 27–28,
46–48; and reasons for divorce, 8–9;
and reconciliation of family, 18, 149,
163, 176; resiliency of, 2; as scapegoat,
149. *See also specific topic*
co-parenting, 68, 144–45
collaborative family law, 84–86
communication, 8, 52; attorney-client,
79–80; and deadly errors, 140, 154,
158–68, 170–71, 187–88, 208–11; and
exposing child to adult issues, 208–11;
and presentation of self in court,
133–34; tips about, 167–68; and types
of custody, 67, 68, 69–70, 72

225

personality, 91; and psychological problems, 90–94; and sexual deviancy, 100; and sexual orientation, 100–102; tips about, 104
Disneyland parent, 180–81, 188
divorce, 4–9, 16*n*, 17–18, 23, 24–25, 27–28, 32

emotional costs, 3, 13, 14, 15, 111, 112–22, 162, 186, 205–6
emotional support, 189–201

family: idealization of and fantasies about, 18–19; living environment of, 97–100; reconciliation of, 18, 149, 163, 176. *See also* demise of family life
financial costs, 64, 99, 136, 186; of child custody warfare, 105–10, 111, 122; and personality, 52, 53, 54, 61, 107. *See also* money
firearms, 100
former spouses: interviews with, 126–27
Frede, Richard, 74
friends, 15, 189–201, 223

Gannon & Cottrell, P.C., 80*n*
grandparents, 190, 198, 200–201, 223
guardian ad litem (GAL), 60, 82, 107, 131

Handschu, Barbara Ellen, 33
"House-Tree-Person Projective Drawing Technique (H-T-P)," 22, 22*n*

willegal drugs, 98
imminent danger, 58
impaired persons, 29, 30, 67, 79, 224; controllers married to, 32, 54–56; impaired persons married to, 32, 34, 56–58; and mediation/negotiation, 34, 79, 84, 87; problem solvers married to, 31, 42–51, 60; recognition of self as, 61–62
in-laws, 198, 200–201
interrogatory questions, 89, 110
"island game," 21, 21*n*, 22

joint custody, 66, 68–71, 84, 144–45, 187
Jost, Kenneth, 69
judges, 86, 91, 97; changing decisions of, 136–38; and costs of custody warfare,

107, 110–11, 113; and custody evaluations, 123, 131; factors considered by, 64–65; functions of, 132–33; interviews of child by, 123, 205–6; respect for, 133–34; time for deliberation/rulings of, 135–36. *See also* court

Kisthardt, Mary Kay, 33

legal representation. *See* attorneys
listening: importance of, 163–64, 168, 179
loyalty issues: and costs of custody warfare, 115; and custody evaluations, 128; and deadly errors, 146, 156, 171–72, 174, 180, 195, 196; and demise of family life, 3; and personality, 60

marital residences, 11–12, 73–75, 205, 221
marriage: child's attitudes about, 27–28; in love with idea of, 4–5; need for effort in, 7–8
marriage counseling, 8, 57, 91–92
mediation and negotiation, 97, 154; and attorneys, 79, 80–82, 84–86; and collaborative family law, 84–86; and denigration of other parent, 83–104; failure of, 84, 87–104; and joint custody, 84; in non-child custody cases, 84; overview about, 83–86; and personality, 33–34, 35, 59, 60, 79, 84, 87, 91
Minton, Michael, 79
money: and deadly errors, 180–81, 188, 203, 206–7, 208–9; and divorce and separation, 10–11; and exposing child to adult issues, 203, 206–7, 208–9; and family's living environment, 99. *See also* financial costs

neighbors, 15, 189–201, 223
new love interests: and abuse, 120; and costs of custody warfare, 120; and custody warfare, 15; and deadly errors, 143, 162, 174, 210–11; and exposing child to adult issues, 210–11; failure of, 15; introducing child to, 212–20; and personality, 42; and types of custody, 75

59188